WHAT YOU NEED TO KNOW ABOUT VOTING—AND WHY

ALSO BY KIM WEHLE

How to Read the Constitution—and Why

WHAT YOU NEED TO KNOW ABOUT VOTING AND WHY

KIM WEHLE

HARPER

NEW YORK • LONDON • TORONTO • SYDNEY

HARPER

HarperCollins books may be purchased for educational, business, or sales promotional use. For information, please email the Special Markets Department at SPsales@harpercollins.com.

FIRST EDITION

Designed by Jen Overstreet

Library of Congress Cataloging-in-Publication Data has been applied for.

ISBN 978-0-06-297478-5 (pbk.)

20 21 22 23 24 LSC 10 9 8 7 6 5 4 3 2 1

For my late parents, Betty Jane Nelson and Richard Edwin Wehle, who taught me about the importance of education and the privilege of having choices in life

Contents

Introduction

The 2020 presidential election is destined to be one of the most critical races in the history of the United States for one glaring reason: it's pivotal for ensuring the integrity of our system of government.

Consider the stakes. You might be rooting for a second term for Donald Trump. Or you might be deeply invested in electing a new president in 2020. Either way, the 2020 election matters. If Donald J. Trump is elected to a second term, some will consider the office of the presidency in ruins, as having become "above the law." If Trump is not elected to a second term, he could face indictment by a Department of Justice headed by a new president. Regardless of how one feels about Donald Trump, a former president in shackles would inflict its own kind of trauma on the reputation of the presidency and on the nation as a whole.

The 2020 race is the first presidential election since 2016. Although people disagree on what to do about foreign assaults on our electoral process, there is no getting around two troubling narratives involving recent presidential elections. Career intelligence officials have concluded that the Russian government hacked into the email servers of the Clinton campaign and the Democratic National Committee. It then enlisted WikiLeaks to publicly dump disparaging information on Hillary Clinton in an effort to influence an election that should have been decided exclusively by American voters. Witness testimony and documents made public in Donald Trump's impeachment also made clear that the president inexplicably withheld military aid to Ukraine while asking the new Ukrainian president to announce an investigation into primary rival Joe Biden for the presidency in 2020. Whether you like Trump-the-man or not, we all must accept that this type of behavior could be the "new normal" for the presidency in the twenty-first century: using the power of office to stay in power.

The 2016 presidential election was also the first in memory in which social media "bots"—created and manipulated by the Russians and other adverse foreign powers—spread false information to regular Americans' Facebook, Twitter, and Instagram accounts in order to manipulate individual votes. American internet users were targeted based on demographics and ideological views—without even knowing that the resulting "information" they considered in casting votes for president was falsely planted in their Google searches. Although former special counsel Robert Mueller completed his investigation into those Russian conspiracies in March 2019, Congress has done little to address the problem. The nasty Russian bots—that is, automated accounts that post lies on social media—are still doing their thing in the lead-up to November 2020. (Note that, as a factual matter, this is not up for debate; Senate intelligence reports as well as the Mueller report document attempts by foreign actors to infiltrate voter registration and other voter data systems in a number of states in 2016).[1]

Meanwhile, a stalemated, polarized Congress has made little progress on other issues that a majority of Americans care about—such as health care, immigration reform, and measured gun control, just to name a few. The reasons for Congress's fecklessness are manifold. They include money in politics, gerrymandering, configuration in the Senate, the absence of term limits, increasingly entrenched partisanship, and a general lack of both courage and political will. There is a major disconnect between the needs and desires of individual voters and how our elected representatives are carrying out their mission in the halls of the legislatures. After the controversial and politically charged confirmation of Justice Brett Kavanaugh to the US Supreme Court, many Americans believe—rightly or wrongly—that the federal courts cannot be trusted or reasonably expected to "fix" what's wrong in American government either.

For most Americans, the sole and pragmatic answer to America's problems lies—if anywhere—at the ballot box. If we want change, we have to vote. But that solution presents its own problems.

For one, few people realize that the Constitution contains no express "right" to vote. Some view it as a privilege to be earned, even for citizens, while others feel it is the heart and soul of American democracy that should be both protected and enhanced more profoundly than any other "right" in America. This pitched battle around whether there's a "right" to vote, or whether only the "right" people should be *able* to vote, lurks below the surface of American consciousness and conversation. But it is real.

Usually, it's couched as a debate over voter suppression (keeping people from the polls) versus voter fraud (impostors going to the polls). What part of this debate is myth and what is reality? How much should Americans have to do to prove that they are eligible to vote on voting day—particularly given that federal criminal laws already create a strong disincentive to fake it at the ballot box? If there is a danger of fraud nonetheless, does that risk outweigh the danger of barring eligible people from having their voices heard in the democratic process? How best to strike that balance? There are no clear answers to these questions, which makes many of us uneasy.

Second, voting in America can be confusing because it can vary depending on where you live. Typically, fewer than 50 percent of eligible voters participate in American elections. Of the thirteen thousand different voting districts across the United States, few do things exactly alike. When it comes to the presidency, the Electoral College means that voters don't even cast a vote for the actual person who could be president. They cast votes for one or more "electors," who then vote for the candidate favored by voters, but voters know little to nothing about electors. Those people aren't legally bound to vote the way the voters say they're "supposed" to, but they usually do. Thus, it's that group of individuals who technically "decide" who will be the next president. Although electors generally go along with what the voters want, for a number of reasons, not all validly cast votes are ultimately impactful in that process.

But this is emphatically *not* to say that people shouldn't bother to vote. Voting is vitally important, even if an individual vote doesn't sway a particular election one way or another. It is the only way that "We the People" self-govern. The ability to self-govern is a privilege and a gift—one that we honor by showing up at the ballot booth, even if your vote doesn't "matter" in altering a particular race. It's sometimes hard for Americans to fathom that not everyone on the planet enjoys the privilege of self-government. If we want to keep that privilege, we need to exercise it. By the end of the first chapter of this book, you will understand how to register and how to vote. (Voting is pretty easy.) And by the end of the book, you will understand why it's extraordinarily important and meaningful, too.[2]

In short, the right to vote is perhaps the most fundamental of our fundamental prerogatives as Americans. But it's the individual states—not the federal government—that make most of the decisions around voting, and they do so without much interference from the Supreme Court. The wide variety of state decisions around voting rights translates into major differences for Americans' ability to vote. It all depends on where you live.

If any of this comes as a surprise, this book is right for you. Although the book focuses primarily on federal elections, the pages that follow lay out answers to questions about voting basics across the board. Consider this one: If you had to change your polling place or register to vote in a new state tomorrow, would you know what to do? For most of us, the answer is probably no. So, Part I of this book explains what you need to know about the right to vote right *now*. Think of it like a cookbook. What recipe do you want to make? Voting in California? Registering in Florida? Look up the recipe, gather the ingredients, and follow the steps. It also talks about how to make your voter registration stick, how to change your registration if you move to another state, and what students should do about voting while away at college.

Part II delves into the background basics of voting. It explains how the right to vote is not an express constitutional right explicitly articulated in the Constitution, but courts have consistently protected the right to vote because without it, the entire structure of government falls apart. This Part also describes who actually gets to legally vote in America and walks through the key ingredients to electing a president and members of Congress—including the thorny matter of the Electoral College.

Part III talks about the holes in what many people assume is their "right" to vote in America, and why that "right" is endangered today. There are structural barriers to voting—including the phenomena known as gerrymandering, Senate malapportionment, money in politics, voter suppression, voter fraud and misinformation, and the dysfunction of voting mechanics. But voting is the only way to fix those problems. Part III covers all these topics, shortly and sweetly, so you have what you need at your fingertips come November.

The book is designed as a guide—for new voters, for would-be voters (youths and people seeking citizenship), and for those of us who have voted for years but wind up scratching our heads when asked about voting specifics. Each chapter begins with a "takeaway box" that gives you the bottom line on what you need to know and next steps, and ends with a list of questions to test your knowledge and for further discussion, if that's of interest to you.

Voting is the cornerstone of democracy. But much like voting, American democracy itself is not a "right" endowed by a higher power. It is a gift that has operated as a beacon of humanity and freedom to the rest of the world. American democracy, embodied in the US Constitution, means that nobody in elected or appointed office gets so much power that people are picked on arbitrarily. It is how "We the People" govern ourselves. If the structure of our government is to survive for our children and grandchildren, we must see to it. The way to do it is by voting, voting, and voting. If voting didn't matter much, foreign governments wouldn't try to influence it. And if voting didn't matter much, we wouldn't see efforts in America to make it harder for certain people to vote. Your vote *does* matter. Here's hoping that this book serves as a tool for use in that epic, honorable, and even sacred feature of American democracy.

PART I

Voting State by State: What You Need to Know *Now*

In Australia, voting in federal and state elections is mandatory for citizens over the age of eighteen. People are allowed to cast a blank ballot, as if in protest. But they can't just blow off voting. If an Australian fails to vote, he may get an email, text message, or letter asking for an explanation. If that person doesn't give a sufficient reason for not voting, he will be fined. If he ignores the notices or fails to pay the fine, he can have his driver's license suspended.

Under this system, 96 percent of eligible Australians are enrolled to vote, and 90 percent actually turn out. Election day is always on a Saturday, and voting centers are well organized and staffed by an independent commission. Voting teams visit prisons, hospitals, and nursing homes to ensure that people in those places cast their ballots too. As one Australian explains, "Voting in Australia is like a party. There's a BBQ at the local school. Everyone turns up. Everyone votes. There's a sense that: We're all in this together. We're all affected by the decision we make today."

Twenty-four nations—including Argentina, Egypt, Singapore, and Turkey—also require their citizens to vote. Among the countries participating in the Organization for Economic Cooperation and Development (which works to solve common economic, social, and environmental problems), the United States ranks twenty-sixth in voter turnout. Belgium, Sweden, and Denmark are at the top of the list alongside Australia; between 80 percent and 90 percent of voters in those countries cast ballots in recent national elections.[1]

Let's break down voting in the United States a bit more.

Four categories of people matter when it comes to voting. The total US population (*category one*), the number of eligible voters (*category two*), the number of registered voters (*category three*), and the number of people who actually vote (*category four*). At the time Americans cast their ballots in the 2016 presidential election, the Census Bureau counted 322.7 million people (*category one*). Of those, 245.5 million were aged eighteen and older and thus potentially eligible to vote in the 2016 presidential election (*category two*). Of the number of eligible voters, 157.6 million—or 64 percent—reported registering to vote (*category three*). Of that population of registered (as distinct from eligible) voters, 86.8 percent turned out in 2016 (*category four*). All told, only 56 percent of the voting-age population ultimately cast a vote.[2]

Pie Chart
56% of the people
in the US vote!

Deciding which system is better—Australia's or America's—depends on what you care about most. In the United States, the government doesn't force free citizens to participate in the electoral process. This keeps government off the backs of those who have no interest in voting and out of their personal lives in that regard. Moreover, nonregistered US voters—people who don't care enough about the issues to bother (or are ignorant about them or cynical about voting in general)—aren't afforded the power to sway electoral outcomes in untoward ways. The uninformed can't be captured by fringe propaganda that, taken to the extreme, risks mob rule rather than thoughtful, measured, policy-based voting. Maybe that's a good thing.

But political scientists have found that, when forced by governments to participate in elections, voters actually become more knowledgeable about the candidates and the issues—and thus more invested in the process of governing themselves. This seems like a good thing too. In Chile, for example, everyone of voting age was automatically registered to vote for the 2013 election. But the country had moved from compulsory to voluntary voting the year before. Despite universal registration, voter turnout dropped in a single election cycle from 87 percent to 42 percent.

In the United States, voter registration is optional. In places that haven't adopted automatic voter registration, like California, you can't expect anybody in the government to do it for you. And because the process varies from state to state, figuring out how to register to vote can be confusing. Accordingly, to even carry a voter registration card means that a person cares somewhat about the right to vote. The problem with the right to vote in America is not with those who register to vote—but with those who don't. There are also problems with those who want to vote, but are somehow stymied, and with what our electoral system does with the votes that are cast. Some votes effectively "count" more than others. But that's not a noble reason to stay home from the polls.

For now, keep this statistic in mind, and ask yourself whether you think something needs to be done about it: in November 2016, *nearly half of eligible American voters failed to participate in choosing their next president.*[3] Why?

There are two tasks to think about when it comes to voting. Let's call them the "Voter Two-Step." Step one is to register. This can be tricky, but usually all you will need is a valid driver's license. The requirements vary by state, so how to register depends on where you live. Step two is showing up at the ballot booth and actually casting a vote. You might need to arrive with a very particular form of identification in order to vote—even if you're registered. Again, what you need depends on where you live.

If you register and show up with the proper ID but the poll workers don't have you down as registered, then what? It may be that you were thrown off—or purged from—the voter rolls without your knowledge. What do you do then? Well, this part of the book talks about those unfortunate happenings too. Bottom line: if you're getting flak about your eligibility to vote on Election Day, demand that you cast what's called a **provisional ballot**. In some states, if you show up to the polls and aren't on the poll books, you can register on the spot and vote. You don't even need a provisional ballot.

Finally, you might be wondering about voting early, voting by mail (by a so-called **absentee ballot**), or what to do if you move to another state or go off to college. In some states—such as Oregon—voters vote exclusively by mail, and their turnout numbers are higher than states without vote-by-mail (or "VBM") voting.[4] The following cookbook has those recipes too. Just find the chapter or chart on what you want to do, identify your locale, and plug and chug away at securing that right to vote.

1

The Two-Step "Recipe" for Voting

Chapter 1 Takeaway Box

- Voter Two-Step:
    1. Register. This varies by state, but you can always go to the DMV.
    2. Vote. Get accurate information and bring the right ID; this also varies by state!
- If you encounter flak at the polls, demand—at a minimum—to cast a provisional ballot!
- Be sure to keep your registration up to date if you move or miss an election cycle.

Although the right to vote is the centerpiece of a functioning United States Constitution, the actual process of voting is carried out at the state and local levels. Figuring out how to register to vote, the location of your particular polling place, the platforms for particular candidates, and even what to bring to the ballot box can be a bit daunting. If you move from one state to another, you may have to start all over again.[1] Often, by the time you realize that you haven't registered, it's too late. The election might be just days away, and perhaps your state requires registration twenty-nine days in advance of an election (as in Florida). But, if you happen to live in California (and twenty other states), you can go right to the polls on Election Day and register on the spot.[2]

Think about this process as the Voter Two-Step. Step one is registering. Step two is actually voting.

Step One: Registering to Vote

Step one in the Voter Two-Step is: register to vote. And if you want to be sure you can vote in November, register right away. There's a chart in the appendix with the "recipes" for registering to vote state by state. Pick the state, figure out what you need, calendar how far in advance of the election you need to register, and go ahead and do it!

Here's a quick tip: if you don't have time to wade through the requirements of your particular state, just make a trip to your department of motor vehicles (DMV)! It turns out that in 1993, Congress passed the National Voter Registration Act, also known as the "Motor Voter Law," which requires states to provide people with the opportunity to register to vote for federal elections at the same time they apply for a driver's license or try to renew one. (The statute requires a broad array of social service agencies to offer voter registration, as well.) Although it technically only applies to federal elections, the law also requires states to send completed applications to state or local election officials. So it effectively works for state and local elections too. Of course, many of us have shown up at the DMV only to be told to go home and rifle through files to find a document we forgot to bring, like a utility bill with our name and address on it. Be sure to do your homework before you go to the DMV for voter registration purposes too. If states don't comply, the statute gives the Department of Justice (DOJ) the authority to sue.[3]

Perhaps most important for your purposes, the statute allows people to register to vote by mail using a common application form. (Who knew, right?) You can find it here in fifteen different languages: https://www.eac.gov/voters/national-mail-voter-registration-form/. Follow the specific instructions for your state. But this form doesn't work for every state. If you live in North Dakota, Wyoming, or one of the US territories (Puerto Rico, US Virgin Islands, American Samoa, and Guam), you *cannot* use the form. New Hampshire uses the form only as an absentee ballot. (Like Idaho and Minnesota, it allows same-day voting so you don't even need to register in advance.) Also, many states allow you to register to vote online—you can do it from home![4]

Another quick tip: at least three interactive websites—www.vote411.org, https://turbovote.org, and rockthevote.org—allow voters to enter an address and pull up a wealth of information and services, from registering to vote to figuring out your voting registration status to finding a polling place. Run by the League of Women Voters, www.vote411.org even allows you to create a personal ballot by "comparing candidates' positions side-by-side" in advance of going to the polls.[5] The US government also has official websites for this purpose; you can find them here: https://www.usa.gov/register-to-vote, at https://www.eac.gov, or at https://vote.gov.

If you don't want to go online, this book also lists the deadlines for registering in your state, where and how to register, and whether your state has a caucus or primary. It also identifies where to look to find information on candidates in advance of voting day. So take a look at pages 216 to 235 of the appendix for a chart with your own state's registration requirements. ***(Note that, although this information reflects registration requirements as of the date the book***

went to print, the requirements are subject to change, and often do. It is best to call or check online to confirm your state's current requirements so you have the most accurate information possible.)

Step Two: Voting on Election Day

Although you may have registered to vote on time, actually showing up at the correct polling place with the proper identification is a different process. It's also a good idea to review the candidates and their platforms before you go. The best place to do that is on an official government or candidate website—not on social media, where the "Wild West of Falsehoods" lurks. This book tells you what you need to bring on voting day and where to go for information about the candidates and last-minute details. (Again, no guarantees that the information is 100 percent accurate on the date you go to the polls—best to double-check your secretary of state's website or the website for your state or county board of elections for the most up-to-date information. You can start here: https://www.eac.gov/voters/register-and-vote-in-your-state/).

Take a look at pages 236 to 252 of the appendix for a chart listing your own state's requirements regarding what sort of identification (if any) you need to bring to the polls on Election Day (as of the date of publication). Pages 253 to 255 of the appendix contain a chart providing which states allow same-day registration and the requirements for doing so.

If you can't get to the polls on Election Day, your state might let you vote during a specified **early voting period**. Unlike for absentee voting, which I discuss later, you don't need an excuse to vote early. (Some states allow you to physically cast your absentee vote early if the polls are open early. For that, you still need to get an absentee ballot. The only difference is that you cast it at the polling place instead of through the mail).

The time periods for early voting vary by state, and don't necessarily line up as you'd expect. (I know from experience in Maryland that by the time I showed up to vote early, a few days before the election, the polls had closed. I was too late to be early!)[6]

Here's a chart that lists whether your state allows early voting and the time frames for doing so:

STATE	EARLY VOTING ALLOWED?
Alabama	No
Alaska	Yes 15 days before election until day of election
Arizona	Yes 26 days before election until Friday before election
Arkansas	Yes 15 days before election until 5 P.M. Monday before election
California	Yes 29 days before election until day before election

STATE	EARLY VOTING ALLOWED?
Colorado	Yes
Connecticut	No Must be sent by 7 P.M. the day before election
Delaware	Yes At least 10 days before election until Sunday before election
District of Columbia	Yes 7 days before election until Saturday before election
Florida	Yes 10 days before election until 3 days before election
Georgia	Yes Fourth Monday prior to a primary election until Friday immediately prior to election
Hawaii	Yes 10 days before election until Saturday before election
Idaho	Yes Third Monday before election until 5 P.M. Friday before election
Illinois	Yes 40th day before election for temporary polling locations and 15th day before election for permanent locations until end of the day before election
Indiana	Yes 28 days before election until noon day before election
Iowa	Yes 29 days before election until 5 P.M. day before election

STATE	EARLY VOTING ALLOWED?
Kansas	Yes 20 days before election or Tuesday before election (depends on county) until noon day before election
Kentucky	No
Louisiana	Yes 14 days before election until 7 days before election
Maine	Yes 30 to 45 days before election until 3 business days before election
Maryland	Yes Second Thursday before election until Thursday before election
Massachusetts	Yes 11 days before election until second business day before election (Friday before)
Michigan	Yes 40 days before election until day before election
Minnesota	Yes 46 days before election until 5 P.M. day before election
Mississippi	No
Missouri	No
Montana	Yes 30 days before election until day before election
Nebraska	Yes 30 days before election until Election Day
Nevada	Yes Third Saturday preceding election until Friday before election

STATE	EARLY VOTING ALLOWED?
New Hampshire	No
New Jersey	Yes 45 days before election until 3 P.M. day before election
New Mexico	Yes Third Saturday before election until Saturday before election
New York	Yes 10th day before election until second day before election
North Carolina	Yes Third Wednesday before election until 1 P.M. on last Saturday before election
North Dakota	Yes 15 days before election until day before election
Ohio	Yes 28 days before election until 2 P.M. Monday before election
Oklahoma	Yes Thursday preceding election until 2 P.M. on Saturday before election
Oregon	No
Pennsylvania	No
Rhode Island	No
South Carolina	No

STATE	EARLY VOTING ALLOWED?
South Dakota	Yes 45 days before election until 5 P.M. day before election
Tennessee	Yes 20 days before election until 5 days before election
Texas	Yes 17 days before election until 4 days before election
Utah	Yes 14 days before election until Friday before election
Vermont	Yes 45 days before election until 5 P.M. day before election
Virginia	Yes Second Saturday before election until 5 P.M. Saturday before election
Washington	No
West Virginia	Yes 13 days before election until 3 days before election
Wisconsin	Yes 14 days before election until Sunday before election
Wyoming	Yes 40 days before election until day before election

But what if you show up at the wrong polling place (even if you believe it's the right one)? If you show up at a polling place and the staff questions your eligibility to vote—your name isn't on the voter rolls, you don't have the proper identification with you, or a poll watcher challenges your right to vote, for example—the election official *must* offer you a provisional ballot in lieu of a regular ballot.

Within days of an election, election officials will determine whether voters who cast provisional ballots were eligible to vote. Provisional voting is a safeguard against voter disenfranchisement. It's a requirement of a federal statute called the Help America Vote Act of 2002, or HAVA. *Bottom line: never leave a polling place without casting a provisional ballot.*[7]

That said, like most things having to do with voting requirements, whether you can cast a provisional ballot—and whether your ballot will make a difference—depends on where you live. States have different requirements for when and how provisional ballots are counted. Idaho, Minnesota, and New Hampshire do not provide provisional ballots at all (they are exempt from having to provide provisional ballots because they allow voters to register at the polls on Election Day). And some states require voters to follow up on their provisional ballot voting in order for the ballots to be counted. In Maryland, for example, if a voter must cast a provisional ballot due to improper identification, she has until 10 A.M. on the second Wednesday after the election to provide proper ID to a local board of elections.[8]

Here's a chart with more information on provisional voting in your state, as well as how to confirm whether or not your provisional ballot will be counted:

STATE	IS IT ALLOWED?	WILL IT BE COUNTED?	WHERE/HOW YOU MAKE SURE IT'S COUNTED
Alabama	Yes	Yes, as long as it is cast in the correct precinct.	If there was an issue with the voter's identification, the voter must provide proper identification to the board of registrars no later than 5 P.M. on the Friday following Election Day. Voters can contact their local board of registrars starting a week after Election Day to determine if their ballots were counted.

STATE	IS IT ALLOWED?	WILL IT BE COUNTED?	WHERE/HOW YOU MAKE SURE IT'S COUNTED
Alaska	Yes	Yes, even if the voter went to the incorrect precinct (but only the votes for the races in which the voter was eligible to vote in will be counted).	No additional steps are required beyond completing the provisional ballot. A letter is sent to the voter if the ballot is rejected or only partially counted.
Arizona	Yes	Yes, even if the voter went to the incorrect precinct (but only the votes for the races in which the voter was eligible to vote in will be counted).	If there was an issue with the voter's identification, the voter must provide it by returning to the polling place on Election Day before 7:00 P.M. or going to the county elections office within 5 days of Election Day. Voters can check the status of their provisional ballot here: https://voter.azsos.gov/VoterView/ProvisionalBallotSearch.do.
Arkansas	Yes	Yes, even if the voter went to the incorrect precinct (but only the votes for the races in which the voter was eligible to vote in will be counted).	No additional steps are required beyond completing the provisional ballot. In most cases, the election commission will mail a notice to voters notifying them of whether or not their vote was counted.

STATE	IS IT ALLOWED?	WILL IT BE COUNTED?	WHERE/HOW YOU MAKE SURE IT'S COUNTED
California	Yes	Yes, even if the voter went to the incorrect precinct (but only the votes for the races in which the voter was eligible to vote in will be counted).	No additional steps are required beyond completing the provisional ballot. Voters can find the necessary information to check the status of their provisional ballot here: https://elections.cdn.sos.ca.gov/ballot-status/index.htm.
Colorado	Yes	Yes, even if the voter went to the incorrect precinct (but only the votes for the races in which the voter was eligible to vote in will be counted).	No additional steps are required beyond completing the provisional ballot. The election judge will give the voter a receipt that contains directions for the voter to determine the status of the voter's ballot.
Connecticut	Yes	Yes, as long as it is cast in the correct precinct.	No additional steps are required beyond completing the provisional ballot. The moderator will give the voter a receipt that contains directions for the voter to determine the status of the voter's ballot.
Delaware	Yes	Yes, as long as it is cast in the correct precinct.	No additional steps are required beyond completing the provisional ballot. Voters can check the status of their provisional ballots here: https://ivote.de.gov/provotestat.aspx.

STATE	IS IT ALLOWED?	WILL IT BE COUNTED?	WHERE/HOW YOU MAKE SURE IT'S COUNTED
District of Columbia	Yes—referred to as "special ballots"	Yes, even if the voter went to the incorrect precinct (but only the votes for the races in which the voter was eligible to vote in will be counted).	If there is an issue with the voter's identification or proof of residence, the voter has 2 days to show proper identification/ proof of residence to the board of elections. Voters can check the status of their ballots here: https://www.dcboe.org/Voters/Absentee-Voting/Special-Ballot-Status.
Florida	Yes	Yes, as long as it is cast in the correct precinct.	The voter must provide evidence of voter eligibility to the local supervisor of elections no later than 5 P.M. on the second day following Election Day. If the sole reason for casting the provisional ballot was due to a lack of proper identification, the voter does not need to provide further evidence. The signature on the provisional ballot will be compared to the signature on file with the local canvassing board. Voters will receive a Notice of Rights at the polling place with instructions on how to check the status of their ballots.

STATE	IS IT ALLOWED?	WILL IT BE COUNTED?	WHERE/HOW YOU MAKE SURE IT'S COUNTED
Georgia	Yes	Yes, even if the voter went to the incorrect precinct (but only the votes for the races in which the voter was eligible to vote in will be counted).	If there is an issue with the voter's identification, the voter has 3 days from the close of voting to provide proper identification to the county registrar office. Voters can check the status of their provisional ballots here: https://www.mvp.sos.ga.gov/MVP/mvp.do.
Hawaii	Yes	Yes, as long as it is cast in the correct precinct.	No additional steps are required beyond completing the provisional ballot. Voters can check the status of their ballots by calling 1-808-453-VOTE (8683).
Idaho	No	N/A	N/A
Illinois	Yes	Yes, as long as it is cast in the correct precinct.	If there is an issue with the voter's identification, the voter has until 7 P.M. on the Thursday following Election Day to provide proper identification to the county clerk's office. Voters can check the status of their ballots on their county clerk's website (starting 2 weeks after Election Day).

STATE	IS IT ALLOWED?	WILL IT BE COUNTED?	WHERE/HOW YOU MAKE SURE IT'S COUNTED
Indiana	Yes	Yes, as long as it is cast in the correct precinct.	No additional steps are required beyond completing the provisional ballot. Voters may contact the county election board after Election Day to determine if their ballots were counted.
Iowa	Yes	Yes, as long as it is cast in the correct precinct.	The voter may provide evidence of voting eligibility to the precinct election officials or the county auditor's office by the date listed on the provisional ballot envelope. Voters can check the status of their ballots here: https://sos.iowa.gov/elections/absenteeballotstatus/absentee/search.
Kansas	Yes	Yes, even if the voter went to the incorrect precinct (but only the votes for the races in which the voter was eligible to vote in will be counted).	The voter must complete both a voter registration application form and the provisional ballot. Voters may contact the local county election office after Election Day to determine if their ballots were counted.
Kentucky	Yes	Yes, as long as it is cast in the correct precinct.	No additional steps are required beyond completing the provisional ballot. Voters can check the status of their ballots here: https://vrsws.sos.ky.gov/provweb/.

STATE	IS IT ALLOWED?	WILL IT BE COUNTED?	WHERE/HOW YOU MAKE SURE IT'S COUNTED
Louisiana	Yes	Yes, even if the voter went to the incorrect precinct (but only the votes for the races in which the voter was eligible to vote in will be counted).	No additional steps are required beyond completing the provisional ballot. Voters can check the status of their ballots here, starting one week after Election Day: https://voterportal.sos.la.gov/provisionalvoters.
Maine	Yes	It depends—voting officials count all ballots first, and the validity of provisional ballots is only investigated if the number of provisional ballots cast would change the outcome of the election.	No additional steps are required beyond completing the provisional ballot. A notice will be posted on the Maine Department of the Secretary of State website to let voters know if provisional ballots have been investigated.
Maryland	Yes	Yes, even if the voter went to the incorrect precinct (but only the votes for the races in which the voter was eligible to vote in will be counted).	If there is an issue with the voter's identification/proof of residency, the voter must provide proper identification/proof of residency to their local board of elections by the second Wednesday after the election. Voters can check the status of their ballots here: https://voterservices.elections.maryland.gov/VoterSearch

STATE	IS IT ALLOWED?	WILL IT BE COUNTED?	WHERE/HOW YOU MAKE SURE IT'S COUNTED
Massachusetts	Yes	Yes, even if the voter went to the incorrect precinct (but only the votes for the races in which the voter was eligible to vote in will be counted).	If there is an issue with the voter's identification, the voter must provide proper identification to the polling place or office of their local election official by the close of voting on Election Day. Voters can check the status of their ballots by calling 1-800-462-VOTE (8683).
Michigan	Yes	Yes, as long as it is cast in the correct precinct.	If the voter failed to provide proper identification or residency verification, the voter must provide it to their local city or township clerk no later than 6 days after Election Day. Voters can contact their local city or township clerk to determine the status of their ballots.
Minnesota	No	N/A	N/A
Mississippi	Yes	Yes, as long as it is cast in the correct precinct.	No additional steps are required beyond completing the provisional ballot. Voters will receive written information at the polls regarding how to determine if their ballots were counted.

STATE	IS IT ALLOWED?	WILL IT BE COUNTED?	WHERE/HOW YOU MAKE SURE IT'S COUNTED
Missouri	Yes	Yes, as long as it is cast in the correct precinct.	If the voter failed to provide proper identification, the voter must provide it to the election officials at the polling place before the close of polls on Election Day. Your provisional ballot will be counted if you return to the polling place and show an Option 1 ID or if the signature on the provisional ballot envelope matches the signature on your voter registration record. Voters will receive written information at the polls regarding how to determine if their ballots were counted.
Montana	Yes	Yes, as long as it is cast in the correct precinct.	The voter has until 5 P.M. on the day after Election Day to provide valid identification or voter eligibility information to the county election office. Voters will be notified by election officials regarding whether or not their ballots were counted.

STATE	IS IT ALLOWED?	WILL IT BE COUNTED?	WHERE/HOW YOU MAKE SURE IT'S COUNTED
Nebraska	Yes	Yes, as long as it is cast in the correct precinct.	No additional steps are required beyond completing the provisional ballot. Voters can check the status of their provisional ballots starting the second Wednesday after Election Day here: https://www.votercheck.necvr.ne.gov/.
Nevada	Yes	Yes, as long as it is cast in the correct precinct.	No additional steps are required beyond completing the provisional ballot. Voters can call 1–877-766-8683 to check the status of their provisional ballots starting the eighth day after Election Day. Voters will need their unique affirmation number that they received at the polling place.
New Hampshire	No	N/A	N/A
New Jersey	Yes	Yes, even if the voter went to the incorrect precinct (but only the votes for the races in which the voter was eligible to vote in will be counted).	No additional steps are required beyond completing the provisional ballot. Voters can call 1-877-658-6837 to check the status of their provisional ballots.

STATE	IS IT ALLOWED?	WILL IT BE COUNTED?	WHERE/HOW YOU MAKE SURE IT'S COUNTED
New Mexico	Yes	Yes, even if the voter went to the incorrect precinct (but only the votes for the races in which the voter was eligible to vote in will be counted).	No additional steps are required beyond completing the provisional ballot. Voters can check the status of their provisional ballots here: https://voterportal.servis.sos.state.nm.us/ProvisionalSearch.aspx.
New York	Yes	Yes, even if the voter went to the incorrect precinct (but only the votes for the races in which the voter was eligible to vote in will be counted).	No additional steps are required beyond completing the provisional ballot. The poll worker will give voters a phone number or a website to check the status of their provisional ballots.
North Carolina	Yes	Yes, as long as it is cast in the correct precinct.	No additional steps are required beyond completing the provisional ballot. Voters can check the status of their provisional ballots here: https://vt.ncsbe.gov/RegProvPIN/.
North Dakota	No—provisional ballots are not necessary since voter registration is not required.	N/A	N/A

STATE	IS IT ALLOWED?	WILL IT BE COUNTED?	WHERE/HOW YOU MAKE SURE IT'S COUNTED
Ohio	Yes	Yes, even if the voter went to the incorrect precinct (but only the votes for the races in which the voter was eligible to vote in will be counted).	If the voter did not provide valid identification at the polls, then they must provide it, in person, to the board of elections within 7 days of Election Day. No information is available on how voters can check the status of their provisional ballots.
Oklahoma	Yes	Yes, as long as it is cast in the correct precinct.	No additional steps are required beyond completing the provisional ballot. Voters can contact the county election board to check the status of their provisional ballots after 1 P.M. on the Friday after Election Day.
Oregon	Yes	Yes, even if the voter went to the incorrect precinct (but only the votes for the races in which the voter was eligible to vote in will be counted).	No additional steps are required beyond completing the provisional ballot. Voters can check the status of their provisional ballots here: https://secure.sos.state.or.us/orestar/vr/showVoterSearch.do.

STATE	IS IT ALLOWED?	WILL IT BE COUNTED?	WHERE/HOW YOU MAKE SURE IT'S COUNTED
Pennsylvania	Yes	Yes, even if the voter went to the incorrect precinct (but only the votes for the races in which the voter was eligible to vote in will be counted).	No additional steps are required beyond completing the provisional ballot. Voters can check the status of their provisional ballots starting 7 days after Election Day here: https://www.pavoterservices.pa.gov/Pages/ProvisionalBallotSearch.aspx.
Rhode Island	Yes	Yes, even if the voter went to the incorrect precinct (but only the votes for the races in which the voter was eligible to vote in will be counted).	The voter has until the close of business on the day after Election Day to provide valid identification or additional eligibility information to the Board of Canvassers. Voters can check the status of their provisional ballots here: https://www.ri.gov/election/provisional_ballots/.
South Carolina	Yes	Yes, as long as it is cast in the correct precinct.	No additional steps are required beyond completing the provisional ballot. Voters can check the status of their provisional ballots here: https://info.scvotes.sc.gov/eng/voterinquiry/VoterInformationRequest.aspx?PageMode=ProvisionalBallotInfo.

STATE	IS IT ALLOWED?	WILL IT BE COUNTED?	WHERE/HOW YOU MAKE SURE IT'S COUNTED
South Dakota	Yes	Yes, as long as it is cast in the correct precinct.	No additional steps are required beyond completing the provisional ballot. Voters will receive a notification of whether or not their provisional ballots were counted.
Tennessee	Yes	Yes, as long as it is cast in the correct precinct.	Voters have 2 business days after Election Day to provide proper identification to the election commission office. Voters can contact the Tennessee secretary of state to find out the status of their provisional ballots.
Texas	Yes	Yes, as long as it is cast in the correct precinct.	Voters have 6 days after Election Day to provide valid identification to the voter registrar's office. Voters will receive a notice in the mail regarding whether or not their provisional ballots were counted.
Utah	Yes	Yes, even if the voter went to the incorrect precinct (but only the votes for the races in which the voter was eligible to vote in will be counted).	No additional steps are required beyond completing the provisional ballot. Voters can check the status of their provisional ballots here: https://votesearch.utah.gov/voter-search/search/search-by-voter/track-mail-ballot.

STATE	IS IT ALLOWED?	WILL IT BE COUNTED?	WHERE/HOW YOU MAKE SURE IT'S COUNTED
Vermont	Yes	Yes, as long as it is cast in the correct precinct.	No additional steps are required beyond completing the provisional ballot. Voters will be notified by their town clerk if their provisional ballots were not counted.
Virginia	Yes	Yes, as long as it is cast in the correct precinct.	Voters have until 12 P.M. on the Friday after Election Day to provide valid identification to their local electoral board. Election officials will provide voters with a phone number to check the status of their provisional ballots.
Washington	Yes	Yes, even if the voter went to the incorrect precinct (but only the votes for the races in which the voter was eligible to vote in will be counted).	No additional steps are required beyond completing the provisional ballot. Voters can check the status of their provisional ballots by contacting their county elections department.
West Virginia	Yes	Yes, even if the voter went to the incorrect precinct (but only the votes for the races in which the voter was eligible to vote in will be counted).	No additional steps are required beyond completing the provisional ballot. Voters can check the status of their provisional ballots here: https://services.sos.wv.gov/Elections/Voter/ProvisionalBallotSearch.

STATE	IS IT ALLOWED?	WILL IT BE COUNTED?	WHERE/HOW YOU MAKE SURE IT'S COUNTED
Wisconsin	Yes	Yes, as long as it is cast in the correct precinct.	Voters must provide proper identification or other eligibility information to the polling place by 8 P.M. on Election Day or to the municipal clerk by 4 P.M. the Friday after Election Day. Voters can check the status of their provisional ballots here: https://myvote.wi.gov.
Wyoming	Yes	Yes, as long as it is cast in the correct precinct.	Voters have until the close of business on the day after Election Day to present proper identification or additional eligibility information to the county clerk. Voters will be given information on how to check the status of their provisional ballots at the polling place.

Finally, every state has **absentee voting**, allowing you to vote by mail. But the rules on who can vote by mail vary by state. Military members and families stationed away from their residence can vote absentee—as can overseas US citizens who used to live in the United States. For the rest of us, it depends. If your state allows you to vote by mail, you first have to get the absentee or mail-in ballot. Some states might require you to give a valid excuse, such as injury, illness, disability, or business travel.[9]

Here's a chart on absentee voting to get you started:

STATE	REQUIREMENTS TO APPLY FOR AN ABSENTEE BALLOT
Alabama	• Absent from county on Election Day • Illness or physical disability that prevents you from physically voting at the polling place • Registered Alabama voter but you are *temporarily* living outside the county (military, employed outside of US, in college) • Appointed election officer at a place other than your polling place • You work a required shift (10 hours or more) that coincides with polling hours • You are currently incarcerated in prison or jail and have not been convicted of a felony involving moral turpitude • You are a caregiver for a family member to the second degree of kinship by affinity or consanguinity and the family member is confined to his or her home
Alaska	• No excuse required
Arizona	• No excuse required
Arkansas	• Must include a copy of your Arkansas ID with application and preferred method to receive ballot • "Unavoidably" absent from polling place on Election Day • Illness or physical disability preventing you from physically voting at your polling place • Member of the armed forces or a spouse or dependent of a member of the armed forces • Permanent residence in Arkansas but you are temporarily living outside the United States
California	• No excuse required

DEADLINE FOR APPLICATION	DEADLINE TO RECEIVE BALLOT
In person: 5 days before Election Day By mail: 5 days before Election Day	Received by Election Day
In person: 10 days before Election Day By mail: 10 days before Election Day	Postmarked by Election Day and received 10 days after Election Day
In person: 11 days before Election Day By mail: 11 days before Election Day	Election Day
In person: 1 day before Election Day By mail: 7 days before Election Day By authorized agent: 1:30 p.m. on Election Day	Election Day
By mail: 7 days before Election Day Online: 7 days before Election Day	Postmarked by Election Day and received within 3 days of Election Day

STATE	REQUIREMENTS TO APPLY FOR AN ABSENTEE BALLOT
Colorado	• You will automatically receive a mail ballot as long as you are registered to vote • If you need your ballot mailed to a different address than what is on your voter registration, you must apply
Connecticut	• Absent from town during *all* hours of voting • Illness • Physical disability that makes it difficult for you to physically vote at the polls • Active duty US military • Religion prevents activity on Election Day • Duties as an election official prevent you from voting on Election Day
Delaware	• Business or occupation prevents you from coming to the polls in person • Away at college or university • On vacation • Religion prevents you from coming in person • Experiencing temporary or permanent physical disability • In public service of US or Delaware and cannot come to the polls
District of Columbia	• No excuse required
Florida	• No excuse required • Some counties allow you to request an absentee ballot online (check with supervisor of elections)
Georgia	• No excuse required

DEADLINE FOR APPLICATION	DEADLINE TO RECEIVE BALLOT
By mail: 8 days before Election Day	Received by 7:00 P.M. on Election Day
By mail: 1 day before Election Day	Election Day
By mail: 1 day before Election Day	Election Day
By mail: 7 days before Election Day	No later than 7:00 P.M. on Election Day
In person: 1 day before Election Day By mail: 6 days before Election Day	Election Day
By mail: 4 days before Election Day	Election Day

STATE	REQUIREMENTS TO APPLY FOR AN ABSENTEE BALLOT
Hawaii	• No excuse required
Idaho	• No excuse required
Illinois	• No excuse required
Indiana	• Specific, reasonable expectation you will be absent from the county on Election Day for the entire time the polls are open • Disability • At least 65 years old • Election duties outside of voting precinct • Scheduled to work during the entire time the polls are open • Unavailability of transportation • Confined due to illness or injury • Prevented due to religious discipline or holiday • Participant in state's confidentiality program • Serious sex offender • Member of the military or a public safety officer
Iowa	• No excuse required
Kansas	• No excuse required • Must provide current Kansas driver's license number on application. If you cannot, then you must provide a copy of your photo ID.

DEADLINE FOR APPLICATION	DEADLINE TO RECEIVE BALLOT
By mail: 7 days before Election Day	No later than 7:00 P.M. on Election Day
In person: 4 days before Election Day By mail: 11 days before Election Day	Election Day
In person: 1 day before Election Day By mail: 5 days before Election Day	No later than 14 days after Election Day
In person: 1 day before Election Day By mail: 8 days before Election Day	Election Day
In person: 1 day before Election Day By mail: 10 days before Election Day	Postmarked 1 day before Election Day and received 6 days after Election Day or returned to the county auditor's office by the time the polls close on Election Day
By mail: 7 days before Election Day	No later than 6:00 P.M. on Election Day

STATE	REQUIREMENTS TO APPLY FOR AN ABSENTEE BALLOT
Kentucky	• Advanced in age, disabled, or ill • Military personnel or their dependent • Overseas citizen • Student who temporarily resides outside the county • Voter who temporarily resides outside of Kentucky but maintains eligibility to vote in Kentucky • Incarcerated but not yet convicted of a crime • Employed outside the county during all hours the polls are open
Louisiana	• Student or teacher living outside the parish of registration • Minister, priest, rabbi, or other member of the clergy outside the parish of registration • Are or expect to be temporarily outside the parish of registration on Election Day and during the early voting period • Moved your residence more than 100 miles from your former residence after the voter registration books closed (30 days before Election Day) • Expect to be hospitalized on Election Day and did not know until after early voting had passed or were hospitalized during early voting as well • Expect to be on the water during the election period • Incarcerated not for a felony • Participant in the Confidentiality Program • Sequestered for jury duty on Election Day • Secretary of state, employee of secretary of state, or an employee of the registrar of voters • Age 65 years or older • Reside in a nursing home, veterans' home, or hospital for a physical disability • Involuntarily confined in an institution for mental treatment outside the parish of registration • If you registered to vote by mail, you must vote in person the first time unless you appear in the registrar of voters before Election Day to confirm your identity

DEADLINE FOR APPLICATION	DEADLINE TO RECEIVE BALLOT
By mail: 7 days before Election Day	Election Day
By mail: 4:30 p.m. on the fourth day before Election Day	1 day before Election Day BUT Election Day for hospitalized voters

STATE	REQUIREMENTS TO APPLY FOR AN ABSENTEE BALLOT
Maine	• No excuse required
Maryland	• No excuse required
Massachusetts	• Absent from city or town on Election Day • Physical disability that prevents you from voting at the polling place • Cannot vote at the polls due to religious beliefs • Confined in a correctional facility on something other than a felony charge
Michigan	• No excuse required
Minnesota	• No excuse required
Mississippi	• Will be away from county on Election Day for any reason • Student or teacher at a school that requires you to be away from your county on Election Day • Temporary or permanent disability that makes you unable to vote in person • Parent, spouse, or dependent of a person with a temporary or physical disability who is hospitalized outside of their county or more than 50 miles away and you will be with them on Election Day • 65 or older • Required to be at work on Election Day when the polls are open • Member, spouse, or dependent of the congressional delegation • Disabled war veteran in a hospital • Member of merchant marines or American Red Cross

DEADLINE FOR APPLICATION	DEADLINE TO RECEIVE BALLOT
By mail: 5 days before Election Day	No later than 8:00 P.M. on Election Day
By mail: 7 days before Election Day	Postmarked by Election Day and received 10 days after Election Day
By mail: By 12:00 p.m. on the day before Election Day	Election Day
In person: 1 day before Election Day By mail: 4 days before Election Day	No later than 8:00 P.M. on Election Day
By mail: 1 day before Election Day	Election Day
By mail: 8 days before Election Day	Received 1 day before Election Day

STATE	REQUIREMENTS TO APPLY FOR AN ABSENTEE BALLOT
Missouri	• Will be absent from voting jurisdiction on Election Day • Incapacitated due to illness or physical disability, or caring for such a person • Restricted by religious belief or practice • Employed by Election Day authority • Incarcerated, but retained voting qualifications • Certified participation on the address confidentiality program established under sections 589.660 to 589.681 because of safety concerns
Montana	• No excuse required
Nebraska	• No excuse required
Nevada	• No excuse required
New Hampshire	• Will be absent on the day of any state election • Will be unable to appear due to religious commitment • Unable to vote due to physical disability • Military service • Cannot appear at the polls due to employment obligation during the time the polls are open
New Jersey	• No excuse required

DEADLINE FOR APPLICATION	DEADLINE TO RECEIVE BALLOT
In person: 1 day before Election Day By mail: 7 days before Election Day	Election Day
By mail: By 12:00 p.m. on the day before Election Day	No later than 8:00 P.M. on Election Day
By mail: 11 days before Election Day	Election Day
By mail: No later than 5:00 p.m. on the fourteenth calendar day before Election Day	No later than 7:00 P.M. on Election Day
By mail: No specific deadline but 7 days before Election Day is recommended	Election Day
In person: 3:00 p.m. on the day before Election Day By mail: 7 days before Election Day	No later than 7:00 P.M. on Election Day

STATE	REQUIREMENTS TO APPLY FOR AN ABSENTEE BALLOT
New Mexico	• No excuse required
New York	• Will be absent from county or city on Election Day • Illness or physical disability or caring for such a person • Resident or patient of a Veteran's Health Administration Hospital • Detained in jail awaiting grand jury action or confined in prison after conviction for any offense other than a felony
North Carolina	• No excuse required • Must handwrite signature and if you cannot include a driver's license or social security number, must include a copy of your ID with application • When filling out ballot, must do so in the presence of a notary or two witnesses who must sign the ballot
North Dakota	• No excuse required • Must include a copy of ID
Ohio	• No excuse required • Must provide driver's license number or last four digits of Social Security number. If not, must provide a copy of ID
Oklahoma	• No excuse required
Oregon	• All elections are mail-in • Only apply if you need ballot sent somewhere other than typical mailing address

DEADLINE FOR APPLICATION	DEADLINE TO RECEIVE BALLOT
By mail: 4 days before Election Day	Election Day
In person: 1 day before Election Day By mail: 7 days before Election Day	Postmarked 1 day before Election Day and received 7 days after Election Day
By mail: 7 days before Election Day	Postmarked by Election Day and received no later than 3 days after Election Day
By mail: No specific deadline. 7 days before Election Day recommended.	Postmarked 1 day before Election Day and received 5 days after Election Day
By mail: 3 days before Election Day	Postmarked 1 day before Election Day and received 10 days after Election Day; returned in person no later than 7:30 P.M. on Election Day
By mail: 6 days before Election Day	Election Day
By mail: 5 days before Election Day	Election Day

STATE	REQUIREMENTS TO APPLY FOR AN ABSENTEE BALLOT
Pennsylvania	• Military service • College students • Spouse or dependent of someone in the military • Member of the merchant marine • Member of a religious or welfare group attached to and serving with armed forces • Occupation or duties will cause you to be away from municipalities on Election Day • A war veteran who is bedridden or hospitalized due to illness or injury • Ill or physically disabled • Employed by the commonwealth or federal government and duties require you to be absent • Employed by the county and Election Day duties will prevent you from voting • Observing a religious holiday • Must provide PA driver's license or PennDOT ID number or the last four digits of Social Security number
Rhode Island	• No excuse required

DEADLINE FOR APPLICATION	DEADLINE TO RECEIVE BALLOT
By mail: 7 days before Election Day	For most elections, 5:00 P.M. on the Friday before Election Day; for presidential elections, no later than 8:00 P.M. on Election Day
By mail: 21 days before Election Day	Election Day

STATE	REQUIREMENTS TO APPLY FOR AN ABSENTEE BALLOT
South Carolina	• Will be away from county of residence AND • Student away at college • Serving with American Red Cross or United Service Organization • Government employee • On vacation • Live overseas • Physically disabled • Job prevents you from voting • Certified election official and will be at work • Attending to a sick or disabled person • Admitted to the hospital on day of or at least four days prior • Person who for religious reasons does not want to vote on a Saturday (presidential primaries only) • Death or funeral in your family within three days • On jury duty • 65 or older • Confined to jail or pretrial facility • Member of the armed forces or merchant marines
South Dakota	• No excuse required • Must send a copy of your photo ID with application; if not, must have application signed and notarized

DEADLINE FOR APPLICATION	DEADLINE TO RECEIVE BALLOT
In person: 1 day before Election Day By mail: 4 days before Election Day	Election Day
In person: 1 day before Election Day By mail: 1 day before Election Day	Election Day

STATE	REQUIREMENTS TO APPLY FOR AN ABSENTEE BALLOT
Tennessee	• Will be outside the county of registration • Enrolled as a full-time student outside county of registration • On jury duty • 60 years of age or older • Physical disability and an inaccessible polling place • Hospitalized, ill, or physically disabled • Caretaker of a person who is hospitalized, ill, or disabled • Candidate for office in the election • Election Day official or employee of Election Day commission • Observing a religious holiday • Possess a valid commercial driver license and will be working outside the state or county • Member of the military or overseas citizen • Licensed physician who filed a statement with county election commission stating you are medically unable to vote at least 5 days before Election Day and signed under penalty of perjury. • Reside in a licensed facility providing permanent care other than a penal institution outside county of residence • If you registered to vote by mail, you must vote in person in your first election.
Texas	• 65 years or older • Disabled • Out of the county on Election Day and during the early voting period • Confined to jail but otherwise eligible • If first-time voter and did not provide driver's license number or Social Security number on voter registration, must include copy of photo ID
Utah	• No excuse required

DEADLINE FOR APPLICATION	DEADLINE TO RECEIVE BALLOT
By mail: 7 days before Election Day	No later than the close of polls on Election Day
In person: 11 days before Election Day By mail: 11 days before Election Day	Postmarked by Election Day and received by the day after Election Day
By mail: 7 days before Election Day	Postmarked 1 day before Election Day and received 6 days after Election Day

STATE	REQUIREMENTS TO APPLY FOR AN ABSENTEE BALLOT
Vermont	• No excuse required
Virginia	• Student attending college outside of Virginia locality • Have business outside county/city of residence on Election Day • Personal business or vacation outside residence on Election Day • Working or commuting to work for 11 or more hours between 6:00 A.M. and 7:00 P.M. on Election Day • First responder • Disability or illness • Primarily and personally responsible for the care of a disabled family member confined at home • Pregnant • Confined and awaiting trial, or convicted of a misdemeanor • Electoral board member, registrar, officer of election, or custodian of voting equipment • Religious obligation • Active duty member of the armed forces or merchant marine • Temporarily residing outside of US • Moved to another state less than 30 days before a presidential election • Authorized representative of candidate or party serving inside the polling place • Granted a protective order by a court
Washington	• All elections are mail-in • Only apply if you need ballot sent somewhere other than typical mailing address

DEADLINE FOR APPLICATION	DEADLINE TO RECEIVE BALLOT
In person: 1 day before Election Day By mail: 1 day before Election Day	No later than 7:00 P.M. on Election Day
In person: 3 days before Election Day By mail: 7 days before Election Day	Before the close of polls on Election Day
By mail: No specific deadline; 7 days before Election Day recommended	Postmarked by Election Day and received 5 days after Election Day

STATE	REQUIREMENTS TO APPLY FOR AN ABSENTEE BALLOT
West Virginia	• All registered voters may vote by absentee ballot in person during the period of early voting • May vote by absentee ballot by mail if: • Absent from county due to personal or business travel • Attendance at a college or other place of education • Advanced age or disability and distance from county seat • Employment hours worked • Incarcerated or detained in jail or a home, but not due to a felony, treason, or election bribery • Injury or illness • Inaccessible early voting site and polling place • Personal or business travel and received ballot at address outside the county • Temporary residence outside the county • Served as an elected or appointed state or federal official • In hospital on election day; can have ballot delivered
Wisconsin	• No excuse required • Must submit a copy of valid photo ID unless you are indefinitely confined due to age, illness, infirmity, or disability or military or permanently overseas
Wyoming	• No excuse required

DEADLINE FOR APPLICATION	DEADLINE TO RECEIVE BALLOT
By mail: 6 days before Election Day	Postmarked by Election Day and received by 6 days after Election Day; ballots with no postmark will be counted if received by 1 day after Election Day
By mail: No later than 5:00 p.m. on the Thursday before Election Day	No later than 8:00 P.M. on Election Day
By mail: 1 day before Election Day	No later than 7:00 P.M. on Election Day

DISCUSSION QUESTIONS FOR CHAPTER 1

- Do you feel that the voting registration requirements for your state make sense? Why or why not?

- What about the voter identification or other same-day registration and voting requirements—do they make sense? Why or why not?

- What one thing did you learn from this chapter that you think is worth passing along to others in casual conversation? Why?

2

Moving Out of State, Missed an Election Cycle, or Off to College? An "Ingredient" List for Staying Registered

Chapter 2 Takeaway Box

- Missed an election? Follow up and keep your registration current.

- Moving? Update your address—your registration might not move with you.
- Off to college? Get an absentee ballot from your home state.

Suppose you missed an election cycle, you are moving out of state, you are elderly and recently joined a retirement community, or you are heading off to college. You are already registered to vote in your home state. You may have voted regularly for years, or it may be your first time. There are a number of ways that you might wind up unable to vote if you don't do a little housekeeping.

Moving or Going to College

Whether you are moving within your county, within your state, to another state, to college, or even to another country, here are a few things worth knowing:[1]

- **If I know I'm moving, when should I start thinking about voter registration?** To be safe, if you are moving, take steps to fix your voter registration at least *eight weeks* before an election. Many states have a deadline between two and four weeks before the election, so you don't want to be out of luck because you're out of time.
- **What will I need to change my registration?** Requirements vary, but it's safe to assume that a driver's license, passport, Social Security card, and/or a lease, mortgage, or utility bill with your new address would be helpful items to have handy.
- **Moving within your county?** Update your voter registration form so your address is accurate and you know what polling site to visit on Election Day. You can start here: https://www.usa.gov/register-to-vote, at https://www.eac.gov, or at https://vote.gov. Note that completing a change-of-address form with the US Postal Service or merely changing your address at the DMV won't necessarily do the job.
- **Moving out of your county or state?** Reregister with your new county or state and alert your *prior* state that you have moved, so you can be taken off those rolls. You can only be registered in one state, which is your primary residence. Again, start here: https://www.usa.gov/register-to-vote or at https://www.eac.gov. For states that allow registration using the common federal application form, go here: https://www.eac.gov/voters/national-mail-voter-registration-form/.
- **Taking care of an elderly parent and need to route all mail to your address?** This one is tricky. Not every state allows you to assist other registered voters the way you might need to. You need to figure out where your parent resides or is registered and then call the local election office in that

district. Find out who to contact here: https://www.usa.gov/election-office.

- **I am in the military and will be overseas during the next election. What do I do?** Fill out the Federal Post Card Application (FPCA), available at www.fvap.gov.
- **Going off to college (or your child is)?** If you are going to school in your home state, you can vote in your original polling place (and visit your parents while you're at it). If you want to move the polling place, update your voter registration form so your address is accurate and you know what polling site to visit on Election Day. You can start here: https://www.usa.gov/register-to-vote, at https://www.eac.gov, or at https://vote.gov. If you are moving out of state for college, you can vote by absentee ballot or reregister in the state where you will be attending school, depending on the residency criteria for that state. (This might be a good

idea if you plan to settle there or the new state is a swing state so your vote will count more; otherwise, it might be easier to keep your voter registration in your home state and vote absentee.) Information on voting by absentee ballot can be found at https://travel.state.gov/content/travel/en/international-travel/while-abroad/voting.html, or https://www.fvap.gov. Note that some financial aid sources require you to be a resident of the state you lived in when you applied for financial aid. College students should think carefully about whether or not they want to change their states of registration during college—they should absolutely make sure that a change will not impact their financial aid. Changing your state of residency can also have tax implications. (Once you know you are going to settle somewhere new, the change might make more sense.)[2]

- **If I vote by mail through an absentee or mail-in ballot, do I have to add extra postage for my ballot to get where it needs to go?** Some ballots weigh more than an ounce, which means that a regular stamp won't suffice. The US Postal Service offers special identifiers for envelopes that contain election-related mail. Ideally, your state will take advantage of these services to make absentee voting work. The USPS has experts on hand who can help states design voting materials to enhance efficiency. To learn more, visit https://about.usps.com/gov-services/election-mail/.
- **I'm going abroad for a few years. What now?** You can vote by absentee ballot, but you need to reregister each year with a Federal Post Card Application (FPCA). You can pick one up at a US embassy or consulate, or start the absentee ballot voting process at one of these websites: https://travel.state

.gov/content/travel/en/international-travel/while-abroad/voting.html or https://www.fvap.gov.

- **How do I know the voter registration change actually took effect?** It will probably take a month or two before you get confirmation in the mail of your new registration. You can verify your status online with the National Association of Secretaries of State: https://www.nass.org/can-i-vote. (As we'll discuss in the next chapter, even if you are already registered, it's a good idea to check your status a couple months before an election to make sure your registration is still valid.)

Staying Registered

As we'll discuss in more detail in Part III of the book, every state conducts list maintenance to ensure that voting lists are accurate—

removing people who have died or moved, for example. But they don't always do it correctly or accurately. As a result, it is possible that you will show up on Election Day only to be told that you aren't on the list of registered voters. If that happens, remember that you should always ask for a provisional ballot and vote anyway. If you want to avoid that (as we all do), it's a good idea to verify your registration status online at https://www.nass.org/can-i-vote. This tool will get you to the right website in your state to verify your registration status. (It might be worth making a note in your calendar to do this *eight* weeks before the next election, or by September 1 every year. That way, you have time to fix the problem before Election Day.)

As mentioned before, with fifty states, US territories, and umpteen local jurisdictions to wrestle with, it's impossible to provide totally accurate, up-to-date information in a printed book. But hopefully there's enough here to get you most of the way there. Different states remove people from the ballots for different reasons. Ohio, for example, has purged hundreds of thousands of voters from its rolls for not voting in three consecutive elections. States like Kansas and Iowa (and roughly twenty-eight others) use a program called cross-checking to remove instances of "double voting." This is extremely controversial and unreliable. The minimal search criteria includes two things: your full name and your birthdate. How many people do you think might have your same name or birthday? Imagine being "unregistered" to vote simply because you share a birthday or a name with someone else in those states.

There are a number of other controversial and confusing methods that states use to remove registered voters, and each one is just as troubling as the last. *The safest way to stay registered is to vote in every election you can.* This will help combat systems like the one used in Ohio. Conversely, to avoid removal based on arbitrary government systems, stay up-to-date on your registration status. Log in and confirm that you're registered at three months, two months, and again at one month prior to an election.

Now that we've covered the Voting Two-Step in some detail, the next part of the book turns to why we should all care about voting in the first place. We are all busy people with complicated lives. We rarely do things if the benefits don't outweigh the costs. Why enter a sweepstakes if you know that it's rigged so nobody wins? It's probably not worth your time to scratch off the silver box or collect the decals needed to enter the contest.

Some might argue the same goes for voting. A single vote—particularly in a traditionally "blue" or traditionally "red" state—is not going to change anything. Right? Perhaps. But in massive numbers, votes do make a difference. If that weren't the case, foreign countries would not be trying so hard to infiltrate US elections. Indeed, even in small numbers—as we've seen in prior presidential races—votes can change the course of history. In 2018, the entire balance of Virginia's state legislature was decided by picking a name out of a ceramic bowl when two candidates tied.[3] But more to the point: there are some things we do just because it's right. We pay taxes even though the chances of an audit are extremely slim. We get annual medical exams even though we feel perfectly fine. We are even more vigilant about preventative health care for our children than for ourselves, because they have a long and bright future ahead of them.

Voting is something that we need to do to preserve our individual freedoms for the long term too. It's like tending to an old bridge. If the bricks and mortar wear down, albeit slowly, the bridge could collapse. When that happens, everyone goes down with it—Democrats, Republicans, independents, you name it. A single vote in a single election might be more about which cop gets to direct traffic on the bridge on that day, to be sure. But millions of votes over the course of 230-plus years make the bridge of democracy strong. If you don't like something—anything—about your government, you are hard-pressed to be heard if you don't vote. Or put another way, if you don't vote, you can't complain. (And we all like to complain from time to time, right?)

DISCUSSION QUESTIONS FOR CHAPTER 2

- Now that you know a bit more about how to register and what to bring to the polls, are you more or less convinced that a uniform federal standard would be preferable? Should the US Congress take even a few details about voting off the states' plates and issue national standards for voting (as the Constitution allows it to do)? Or would that be too much of an impediment on states' rights?

- If you could put together a voting "recipe" for yourself and your family right now, what would be in it? Is that recipe something that should go in your important papers file, along with birth certificates and the deed for your home? Why or why not?

- If you aren't convinced that the hassle of voting is worth the effort, what might change your mind? Put another way, what are you hoping to find in this book that you haven't heard already?

3

The Latest on Ballot Confusion and Voting Machine Clunkery

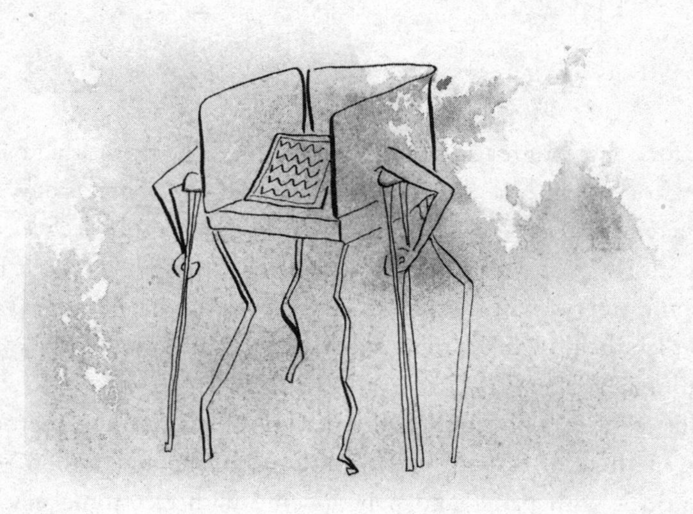

Chapter 3 Takeaway Box

- Ballots vary across the country and can be so confusing that people mistakenly skip voting for certain races or mark their votes incorrectly.

- Voting machines vary from state-to-state and are particularly vulnerable to cyberattacks if they lack paper backups.
- Congress needs to put more funding into voting infrastructure in addition to making Election Day a federal holiday so it's easier to vote. Politics has so far blocked such measures.

Now for a few pragmatic points about voting. The first is that ballots can be confusing. Not all ballots are designed well. Some states send instructions to voters in advance of voting day—a sort of "welcome kit" with FAQs and all. Others do virtually nothing in advance, leaving some voters unaware that an election is even happening. People in the less helpful states may thus be at a disadvantage if they are planning to vote.

Just as there's no single ballot design in this country, there's no single method for actually casting and recording votes either. Some states do it with paper and pencil, some with electronic machinery, some with a little bit of both. Some voting districts don't have enough machines to handle the number of voters efficiently. The point of this chapter is simply to make you aware of these issues so that you can maximize the chance that your own votes register in the way that you intend them to register. Without federal legislation mandating some uniformity regarding the mechanics and hours for voting, however, the only way to improve them is state-by-state and person-by-person.

Ballot Confusion

We all spend a good chunk of our lives filling out forms. Forms—like notices—can be confusing. When parking a car, we might have to puzzle over the signage, especially if there are two or three placards on top of one another, each giving a new tidbit about what hours are legal on what days. If we inadvertently get it wrong, we might come back to find a parking ticket on the windshield. If you grew up in the United States, you might remember the standardized tests in elementary school, where you had to fill in an oval "completely" with a number two pencil. Alongside the instructions there might be an example of a "bad" or "incomplete" bubble fill-in followed by a "good" one. And we've all sat down to play a new board game and felt immediately overloaded by the complex instruction sheet. When you buy online furniture these days, it may come with an offer to pay extra in order to have someone visit your home and actually put the item together for you. Following instructions can be confusing and frustrating—which is why good instruction design is a skill, if not an art.

In Canada, everyone across the country gets a single ballot format every time they vote. It has a black background with white text listing the candidates' names. Below each name is that candidate's political party. And next to each name is a big white circle. All voters need to do is put an "X" in the white circle alongside their candidate of choice. The form is simple, clear, and familiar.

In the United States, ballot design is not uniform. Many of us recall the "hanging chad" debacle in Broward County, Florida, that ultimately led to George W. Bush's 2000 election to the presidency after the Supreme Court refused to allow a local recount in *Bush v. Gore*. Election workers held ballots up to the light in efforts to divine the intent of the chad-puncher—did the voter mean to punch the half-punched or slightly indented hole or was that an error? In 2018, about 3.7 percent—or 30,896—of voters in Broward County wound up missing a vote for the US Senate altogether because that race was tucked in a column under the ballot instructions, which voters often skip. More people voted in that race for the commissioner of agriculture than for their US senator.

Many states have laws requiring certain ballot designs regarding layout, wording, and typeface. New York law requires a "full face" ballot, meaning that all candidates for the same seat must be on the same page. But that has led to problems, too. The full-face rule means that ballots run onto multiple pages—but with perforations between the pages so that the ballot is technically all one page. Voters in 2018 didn't know—and weren't told—that they were supposed to separate the perforations into separate pages. Not only did they miss certain pages, but the understandable failures to tear the perforated pages apart led the machines to jam. This, in turn, led to longer lines.

This sort of nonsense, of course, is avoidable. Experts know how to design good ballots. A few guidelines:

- Leave blank space below the instructions.
- Put the first contest at the top of the next column—not under the instructions.
- Keep ballots short. This may require separate ballots for languages other than English.
- Educate the public about the ballot in advance of the election, perhaps even making a sample ballot available online or sending it by mail with registration cards.[1]

Politics, machinery, budgets, and storage space all come into play in designing ballots—there's no way around the fact that ballot design is complex. Ideally, it should be approached with voter friendliness first and foremost in mind. As I tell my legal-writing students, if a reader has to work to understand what you are saying, you need to go back and try again.

Voting Machine Clunkery

If all else goes well in your exercise of the right to vote, the machinery on Election Day might not. It's often old, inefficient, improperly administered, or ineffective by design. Election officials cannot predict how many people will show up, yet they have to purchase equipment (assuming they even have the funding), staff the polling sites, and estimate how many machines will be needed long before Election Day comes. It's like planning a big party—you never know how many guests will actually come even if you carefully request and track RSVPs. An insufficient supply of working voting machines means longer lines and possibly even disenfranchisement of legitimate voters on voting day.

Across the United States, there are approximately 3,200 counties ranging in size from 100 people (Kalawao County, Hawaii) to around ten million (Los Angeles). The vast majority—more than 70 percent—of these have fewer than fifty thousand residents. Yet each district has to design, administer, and secure a voting process. This effort has become increasingly difficult with technology and cybercrime. Older machines are much less able to sustain the new stresses on voter integrity. The National Academy of Sciences (NAS) has concluded that any voting system that does not also print out voters' choices on paper should be "removed from service as soon as possible." Without a paper trail, votes cannot be verified later. Yet as of 2019, twelve states still use paperless electronic machines in certain counties, and four states—Delaware, Georgia, Louisiana, and South Carolina—use them statewide.

According to a survey conducted by the Brennan Center over the winter of 2018–2019, 121 officials in thirty-one states said that it was "extremely urgent" that they replace their equipment before the 2020 election. Two-thirds of those reported that they didn't have the money to do it. In forty-five states, the voting machines are no longer being manufactured, so it's hard to find the spare parts needed to service and maintain them. Most of the election officials surveyed by the Brennan Center hoped to upgrade their systems with machines that have optical scanners—but not all. One expert noted in dismay, "[W]e need to have a way to independently validate voters' intent away from tabulation equipment. I don't understand how any election official could really consider a totally paperless system in this day and age." Nonetheless, Indiana, Mississippi, Tennessee, and Texas reportedly have no plans to replace their paperless machines before the 2020 election, citing insufficient funding as one reason.[2]

If you reside in a state with old or paperless voting machines, you might consider voting early or by mail-in ballot if your state offers those options. Otherwise, try to show up on Election Day with enough lag time to avoid that jam. (Alas, no guarantees here. In 2012, lines in Florida spanned a seven-hour wait after Republican lawmakers shortened the number of early voting days from fourteen to eight, reportedly in response to "the strong Democratic turnout in early voting in 2008.")[3] Generally, the busiest voting times are first thing in the morning, right before the polls close after the workday, and at lunchtime. Remember, too, that if you are denied the ability to vote for whatever reason on Election Day, ask to cast a provisional paper ballot. And if you find yourself waiting in line at poll-closing time, politely insist that you should still be allowed to vote.

If that doesn't work, try the nonpartisan toll-free hotline operated by the Lawyers' Committee for Civil Rights Under Law: 866-OUR-VOTE (or 866-687-8683). Their website lists hotlines for speakers of other languages, including Spanish and Arabic: https://lawyerscommittee.org/. Professional legal assistance can make a tremendous difference in getting voting problems addressed. In Georgia in 2018, long lines prompted multiple last-minute lawsuits and court orders directing six precincts to stay open longer so that legitimate, diligent voters could actually vote.[4]

Here are a few final tidbits about what to expect on voting day.

Wearing Campaign Gear on Voting Day

Some states limit voters' ability to wear campaign paraphernalia into the voting booth—such as hats, buttons, or T-shirts. If that's your state, polling staff might make you remove the offending item. If you can't take it off or turn a T-shirt inside out, you might find yourself returning home to change clothes before you can vote. Some counties have paper smocks on hand, but don't count on it. Do your campaigning before you go to the polls in order to make sure that your vote goes smoothly on Election Day.[5]

Voters with Disabilities

For certain people with disabilities, the voter challenges we've discussed only get harder. More than 35 million eligible voters—or about one-sixth—have a disability. Without aid, getting to or entering a polling place, reading a ballot, or punching information into a voting machine can be all but impossible. Imagine what it's like to be in a wheelchair facing a locked door, a broken elevator, a ramp so steep that it causes your chair to tip backward, an obstructed pathway to a voting machine that you cannot reach, or a ballot that you cannot see. Imagine, too, that you finally get inside your precinct only to face a poll worker who questions your disability or your eligibility to vote, who talks down to you, or who literally tells you which candidates you should vote for (as if you're not smart enough to decide on your own).[6] Most poll workers perform the very important public service of staffing elections with dedication, integrity, and professionalism. But people with disabilities face obstacles that the rest of the voting population does not.

Studies show, for example, that in 2018 the percentage of visually impaired voters able to cast votes using a problem-free, accessible voting machine was only 59 percent. (In 2008, a much higher 87 percent reported they were able to vote without obstacles.) Machines tended to crash or jam, audio headphones were broken, and voters had a hard time pushing the user interface buttons or finding adequate instructions in Braille. One-third of respondents reported that poll workers had problems with the machines too. Only 21 percent said that workers gave clear assistance.[7]

A federal statute called the Americans with Disabilities Act prohibits states from banning people from voting because of their disability, and another law called the Voting Accessibility for the Elderly and Handicapped Act requires access to voting for individuals aged sixty-five and up and individuals with disabilities. Ballots must be printed in large type and polling stations must include access to telecommunication devices (TDD) for the hearing impaired. If polling places aren't accessible to all people with disabilities, states need to provide an alternative polling place on Election Day. The law also makes clear that voters cannot be required to produce a doctor's note in order to cast an absentee ballot due to disabilities. In 2002, Congress passed another law—the Help America Vote Act (HAVA)—which required each polling place to have an upgraded and accessible voting system by 2006, among other things. The specifics were left to each state.[8]

Of course, laws are only as good as they are enforced. A speed limit of thirty-five means nothing if people routinely cruise down the same road at fifty-five miles per hour without getting a ticket. People will learn that the speed limit is never enforced on that road, and they'll speed. Likewise, laws mandating voter access for the elderly and people with disabilities are only as good as they are enforced. In this instance, the entity charged with enforcement is the Department of Justice. In a study conducted in 2013, the US Government Accountability Office found that 46 percent of the polling stations its staff visited posed problems for disabled voters, including a lack of voting stations that accommodate wheelchairs. The federal government thus conceded that "gaps remained" in its efforts to enforce the laws protecting disabled voters.[9]

So what do you do if you are an elderly or disabled person and concerned about voting on Election Day? Well, the first step is to learn about voting and the particular laws of your state—a step you've already begun if you are reading this book. Even if you are used to being completely independent, consider having someone you trust accompany you to the polling place so that you can get immediate help with whatever additional challenges you might face by virtue of your age or disability. You might also call your polling place in advance, identify your needs, and obtain information about accessibility and options. When you arrive, be sure to ask for whatever help you need. Or as an alternative to showing up at the polls at all, consider early or absentee voting, which many states offer, so that you can obtain and return your ballot through the US mail.

If you experience a problem with accessibility, contact your state or local elections office, or the Department of Justice's Voting Rights Division. You can file a complaint with that office by visiting https://www.justice.gov/crt/complaint/votintake/index.php.[10]

Non-English Ballots

Since the enactment of the Voting Rights Act in 1975, federal law has required that election ballots be printed in languages other than English. Whether states need to do this—and if they do, in what languages—depends on the number of eligible voters who live in a particular community and have both limited English skills and less than a fifth-grade education. The languages most needed include those of people who are of Latino, Asian American, American Indian, and Alaska Native descent. Every five years, the US Census Bureau calculates which areas must meet this requirement. The last count happened in 2016 and identified approximately 263 jurisdictions in twenty-nine states that have to provide ballots in one or more languages other than English. Covered jurisdictions must translate registration materials, information materials, and absentee voting materials—in addition to ballots—into the other language or languages. Most often, the required language is Spanish. But dozens of additional languages are offered across the country, including Apache in Pinal County, Arizona, and Ute in San Juan County, Utah.

As with the other voting laws, these language assistance requirements must be enforced or they become meaningless. From 2011 to 2016, the Department of Justice brought complaints against four jurisdictions for violating the Voting Rights Act, all of which led to consent orders or settlements. As of the fifty-third anniversary of the Voting Rights Act in 2016, however, the Trump administration had not brought any enforcement actions under the statute. In fact, it abandoned the federal government's enforcement positions in at least three voting rights matters—two of which involved alleged intentional discrimination by states on the basis of race.[11]

DISCUSSION QUESTIONS FOR CHAPTER 3

- We see a lot on the news about budgets, price tags for federal programs, and tax cuts. Do you think that spending taxpayer dollars on securing a solid voting infrastructure in the United States should be a priority? Why or why not?

- Has this chapter changed how or when you might plan your vote in the next election? If so, how?

- Technology has put electoral integrity at risk—just as it has done with our own private data, which is vulnerable to cyberattacks just like state voter registration lists are. Can you think of ways to design a ballot or a voting machine to make it safe from sabotage? Is this an area where the technology should go backward, not forward?

PART II

Voting Is *Not* a Constitutional Right (It All Depends)

How did we arrive at a system in which so many of us don't even bother to vote? This Part attempts to answer this question with a few fundamentals about what the US right to vote means in the first place. It starts with the text of the Constitution (which does *not*

include an affirmative "right" to vote), then outlines a few things that the US Supreme Court has had to say about that right. In our three-part national government, Congress has the power to legislate—and it has used it to pass a few laws about voting. This chapter reviews some of those laws too. This Part talks about qualifying to vote—and how that issue gets tricky when it comes to people on the margins of citizenship, such as immigrants and prison inmates. Finally, it outlines some basics about electing a president and members of Congress. What are the key ingredients for each? And what is the gist of the Electoral College, anyway? This is the stuff of core civics, folks. Don't fret . . . I'll try to keep it interesting.

4

What Does the "Right" to Vote Even Mean?

Chapter 4 Takeaway Box

- The Constitution contains no express *right* to vote, but it's central to American democracy and of vital importance.
- The Constitution does contain some language

prohibiting the government from discriminating against certain people by denying them the right to vote.

- The Supreme Court mostly stays out of fights about voting, with a couple notable exceptions.
- Ironically, most voting problems must be fixed by voting to change things—not by lawsuits.

Most Americans understand that they have a "right" to vote. But what does that mean? When thinking about a "right," we might think of a power that cannot be taken away. A right to speech means that the government cannot arbitrarily silence you in one way or another. A right to own a gun means that the government cannot pass a law making it illegal for anyone other than law enforcement or the US military to possess a gun. A right to an abortion means that the government cannot penalize a woman for having an abortion. Likewise, the right to vote must mean at a minimum that the government can't arbitrarily ban people from voting for their federal, state, or local leaders. Right?

But the right to vote is different from other rights identified in the text of the Constitution. Free speech is contained in the First Amendment. Gun rights are in the Second Amendment. What about voting?

Well, it turns out that the US Constitution does not contain language explicitly preserving the right to vote. It doesn't state, for example, that "the right to vote shall not be circumscribed," or anything of the sort. This may come as a surprise, because voting is the foundation for American democracy. It's perhaps the most important right of all rights, because it's ultimately how government infringements of other constitutional or legal rights may be addressed—that is, at the ballot box. If the government goes around violating people's rights, victims can file lawsuits. But barring that, the only recourse is to throw the bad actors out of office. Rules mean nothing without consequences for violating them, and a major consequence for bad deeds by elected leaders in a democracy is losing one's job—because the voters are the ultimate boss of elected officials.

Before we get to the source of the right to vote, let's review some constitutional basics. The original Constitution consists of three articles, each of which corresponds to a distinct branch of government. Article I lays out the powers of Congress, also known as the legislative branch. Article II lists the powers of the president, or the executive branch. Article III is about the judicial branch—the US Supreme Court and the lower federal courts. In addition to the three articles of the Constitution, there are amendments. The Constitution has been amended twenty-seven times so far (including Prohibition, which was repealed).[1]

There is no provision in the Constitution that expressly confers a *right* to vote. But the concept of voting is referenced eight separate times in the Constitution—twice in Article I of the original Constitution (the one about Congress), and six times in amendments to the Constitution. The amendments don't exactly give an affirmative right to vote. Instead, they bar the government from discriminating against certain categories of people by precluding them from voting. Let's run through these in a bit more detail, as they together form the cornerstone of virtually everything that follows in this book.

Here's what the original Constitution says about voting:

- Article I, Section 2 states that the people pick members of the House of Representatives. It also identifies the prerequisites for House membership. Members must be at least twenty-five years old and live in the state they are elected to represent.[2]

- Article I, Section 4 indicates that states—not the federal government—determine how the election process goes. What that also means is that the process can (and does) vary from state to state. In short, how the "right" to vote plays out for you hinges on your zip code.[3] This is not the case for other fundamental rights, like the right to own a handgun for protection in your home under the Second Amendment. As a constitutional matter, the scope of the handgun-in-the-home right does not depend on your state of residence.[4]

Now let's run through the amendments:

- Amendment XIV is the second of the post–Civil War trio. It protects the right to vote for the "male inhabitants of [each] state, being twenty-one years of age, and citizens of the United States." In the original Constitution, states allowing slavery could count each slave as three-fifths of a person for purposes of determining how many representatives they would have in Congress (a process known as "apportionment"). Section 2 of the Fourteenth Amendment repealed the three-fifths clause.[5]
- Amendment XV granted African American men the right to vote in 1870—one of three amendments adopted after the Civil War (including the Thirteenth Amendment's ban on slavery). This is the first time we actually see the words right and vote in the Constitution.[6]
- Amendment XVII changed the way we elect senators. Remember that we talked about Section 2 and Section 4 of Article I. We skipped Section 3 of Article I—because the Seventeenth Amendment made it obsolete. Under the

original Constitution, state legislatures picked senators. The Seventeenth Amendment now provides that senators are elected by the people.[7] (It turns out that, at the time of the Seventeenth Amendment, many states were already allowing voters in primary elections to designate whom they wanted for the Senate, and state legislatures generally went along with the majority preference anyway.)[8]

- Amendment XIX finally gave women the right to vote—on August 18, 1920—barely one hundred years ago as of the date of this book's publication. Like the Fifteenth Amendment, it states that "[t]he right of citizens of the United States to vote shall not be denied or abridged by the United States or by any State on account of sex." Recall that the original Constitution, which was officially ratified in 1788, left the details of voting rights up to the states. At that time, women were only allowed to vote in New Jersey, which revoked the right in 1807.[9]
- Amendment XXIII handed Washington, DC, residents the right to vote for representatives in the Electoral College, which is the method for electing a president of the United States. The language of the Twenty-Third Amendment is not as clear as that of the Fifteenth and Nineteenth Amendments, however. It doesn't speak directly about the right to vote.[10]
- Amendment XXIV prohibited states and the federal government from imposing what's known as a "poll tax" on voters as a precondition to voting in federal elections. The Twenty-Fourth Amendment doesn't ban poll taxes in state and local elections—just federal ones.[11]

A few words of explanation are needed here. Not only did the framers of the original Constitution leave the election process up to the states, but as Part I of the book made clear, they also left voter qualifications up to the states. In 1788, many states only let property owners vote—which mostly meant white men with financial means (few nonwhites and formerly enslaved men also owned property in colonial America). The rationale was that white male property owners had the greatest stake and interest in the outcome of an election. Property ownership later morphed into the requirement that people pay for the right to vote through poll taxes. Poll taxes allowed people without sufficient property ownership to vote. Those who paid the tax were presumably interested in how their tax dollars were used. But by the mid-nineteenth century, poll taxes were mostly dropped for free white men. They only constrained black men. That's where the Fifteenth Amendment came in (we covered this one already, as you will recall).

Immediately following ratification of the Fifteenth Amendment, African Americans' participation in voting, elections, and elected office soared—for a time. Starting in 1889, all the states that had been part of the Confederacy during the Civil War started imposing restrictions on voting, such as literacy tests and poll taxes. Historical records indicate that these constraints sprang from a desire to keep African Americans from voting. The voter suppression efforts worked, affecting not only the black vote, but also that of low-income white men. Many states allowed poll taxes to accumulate year after year, so that an overdue tax bill made it virtually impossible for some people to reclaim their ability to vote. By 1962, poll taxes remained in Alabama, Arkansas, Mississippi, Texas, and Virginia. The Twenty-Fourth Amendment was ratified to obliterate poll taxes in

1964, two years after it passed Congress and in the midst of the civil rights movement.[12] (Voter suppression efforts are further evidence that your vote matters—if it didn't, legislatures wouldn't bother trying to make it harder for certain people to vote.)

- Amendment XXVI is the last entry of constitutional provision bearing on the right to vote. Recall that the Fourteenth Amendment protects voting rights for citizens twenty-one and older. It does not prohibit states from allowing younger people to vote, but forbids states from barring people eighteen and older from voting. Prior to the Twenty-Sixth Amendment, most states imposed a twenty-one-year-old limit, which became a problem during the Vietnam War. Younger men were sent to fight and die on the battlefield, but they could not cast a vote for or against the elected officials who effectively had the power to decide their fate. Congress tried to fix this problem by statute in 1970, but the Supreme Court held in a case called *Oregon v. Mitchell* that Congress had no power to lower the voting age in state and local elections—only federal elections.[13] The Twenty-Sixth Amendment followed, prohibiting states and the federal government from denying people the right to vote based on age.[14]

As with any part of the Constitution, the Supreme Court's interpretation of the document's ambiguous language has profound implications for the scope of the Constitution itself. Consider two important points about what the Supreme Court has ruled regarding voting rights.

The first is that voting is important not because the right to vote appears in the Constitution (it doesn't), but because voting preserves all other constitutional rights. It's the linchpin for everything else. As far back as 1886, the Supreme Court has repeatedly declared that the right to vote is "fundamental" because it is "preservative of all rights."[15] Without the right to vote, individuals can't hold government officials accountable for breaking other laws.

Imagine an antibullying rule in a middle school. If kids can bully without consequences, the "no bullying" rule becomes meaningless. Same with constitutional rights. One important check on government abuses of power, in addition to lawsuits, is through voting. Otherwise, government officials become above the law and their bad behavior won't stop.

When it comes to the right to vote, the second big takeaway from the Supreme Court is the "one person, one vote" rule. Basically, the Supreme Court held that legislative districts—whether at the congressional, state, or local level—must be drawn up so that they each have an *equal population of voters*. Otherwise, if a hypothetical "District Rural" has one thousand voters, and "District Urban" has one million voters—but both can only send one representative to the legislature—then the votes of people in District Rural count a lot more than votes from people in District Urban. District Rural voters will be courted more by candidates. The effect is to marginalize or even silence the views of voters in District Urban. That's unfair. The Supreme Court has decided a bunch of cases on this issue, but the most important one is *Reynolds v. Sims*,[16] in which the court in 1964 held that Alabama's disparities among state legislative districts—with some having forty-one times as many eligible voters as others—was unconstitutional. The court concluded that it's unfair to weigh votes differently based on where people happen to reside. (One important caveat, which we will return to in Part III, is that under the Constitution, the Senate is by definition *dis*proportionate.)

DISCUSSION QUESTIONS FOR CHAPTER 4

- What does it mean to have a "right" to do something? Did this chapter change your views on the robustness of your "right to vote" in America?

- How much should the federal government step in to protect the right to vote? Did the framers of the Constitution get it right in leaving voting rights mostly up to states?

- If you could tweak that division of power, how might you do so? Would you have Congress do more to standardize the voting process in the United States? If so, what? Would you object, for example, to a federal law requiring the use of a uniform form of ballot in all elections, like Canada has?

5

Who Gets to Vote Legally in America

Chapter 5 Takeaway Box

- Citizens eighteen years of age and older can vote, but states can impose certain additional restrictions.

- Congress has forbidden noncitizens from voting in federal elections. Most state and local elections also ban noncitizen voting.
- Because of registration requirements, it's hard for homeless people to vote.
- People with felony records may or may not be able to vote, depending on the state.

The Constitution basically says that people who are born here or become a citizen and are aged eighteen or older can vote. States can impose a bunch of other requirements, including residency in the state, but they can't prevent people from voting on the basis of race, color, sex, or age.

As far as additional limitations on voting eligibility by states, this next one is hard to grasp, but here it goes: Article I, Section 2 of the US Constitution states that "the electors in each state shall have the qualifications requisite for electors of the most numerous branch of the state legislature." This language is known as the "Qualifications Clause." What it means is that each state gets to decide the qualifications for voting (along with most everything else about voting, to be honest, except for the Constitution's amendments banning certain voting restrictions based on gender, age, income, and race). The Supreme Court has explained that, at the Constitutional Convention in 1787, "[t]he state governments represented at the Convention had established varying voter qualifications."[1] It was decided that those qualifications would carry over to federal elections. (A national voting standard was a constitutional deal breaker because people felt so strongly about allowing states to keep their way of doing things. The framers compromised—something that our current Congress has mostly forgotten how to do.)

As a result, if you are qualified to vote for members of the lower legislative chamber of your particular state (i.e., the state equivalent of the federal House of Representatives), then you can vote for members of the federal House of Representatives too. According to the Supreme Court, "the Qualifications Clause was intended by the Framers to prevent the mischief which would arise if state voters found themselves disqualified from participation in federal elections." What's good for the states is good for the feds. But even the Constitution says that the opposite isn't the case—federal qualifications do not have to "be at all times precisely equivalent" to state ones.[2]

Recall again that in 1993, Congress did do something important about voting. It passed the Motor Voter Law, which imposed certain voter registration requirements across the board for federal elections.[3] Most significantly, that law requires state governments to allow qualified voters to register to vote when applying for or renewing a driver's license at state motor vehicle agencies, or when seeking social services, such as disability assistance. It also requires states to allow voter registration by mail-in applications, and imposes rules requiring states to maintain accurate and current voter registration lists.[4]

We've been talking all along about how the states get to decide on voter registration requirements. So how is the Motor Voter Law even constitutional? After all, it imposes *national* registration requirements on the vast majority of the states. Well, under Article I, Section 4 of the Constitution (which was the second of our list of eight places in the Constitution where voting is addressed), "Congress may at any time by Law make or alter such Regulations" prescribed by states.[5] The ins and outs of this analysis can rapidly get too wonky for this book—just know that states prescribe voter registration qualifications, but Congress has set baseline requirements that all states must follow. And as for the particular registration requirements for your state, check out the chart in the Appendix.

A few final words about the voting rights of certain categories of traditionally disenfranchised people: immigrants, homeless individuals, and people with current or past felony convictions (those who are incarcerated as well as those who have completed their sentences, are on probation, or are on parole). The rights of these people can vary state-by-state.

Noncitizens

Under a law passed by Congress in 1996, noncitizens cannot vote in *federal* elections. Illegal immigrant voting is relatively rare. If it occurs, the Illegal Immigration Reform and Immigrant Responsibility Act of 1996 authorizes the federal government to impose fines, imprisonment, and deportation.[6] There is no federal law prohibiting noncitizens from voting in *state or local* elections, however. Historically, the ability of noncitizens to vote at the state and local level has varied. At times, allowing noncitizens to vote was perceived as advantageous for the broader US population. During the Civil War, for example, the Union army needed help, so the government began drafting people based on noncitizen voting rights. Today, most states and local governments ban noncitizen voting, although that might be changing. Since 2008, for example, a number of local municipalities in Maryland have enabled foreigners to vote in their elections under the premise that increased turnout by folks who live in the community (despite not being citizens) will result in better, more reflective public policy and legislation.[7]

Homelessness

Homeless citizens face considerable obstacles in exercising their right to vote due to the lack of a mailing address and personal identification, as well as state residency and voter registration requirements.[8] More than 1 percent of the total US population are homeless. Yet research has also shown that when low-income people turn out to vote in higher numbers, increased government spending on welfare benefits follows. In 2014, exit data from midterm elections indicated that "[t]hose making under $50,000, who account for 48 percent of the population, make up only 36 percent of voters, while those making over $100,000 made up 30 percent of voters, but only 22 percent of the population." This disparity among rich and poor voters is not unique to the United States. But the barriers to voting that exist for the homeless and the poor in the United States are unique, in part because most European countries issue free national ID cards and have compulsory voter registration.[9]

Felony Convictions

Since the founding of this country there have also been laws restricting the voting rights of people with felony convictions. Recall that wealthy white male property owners—an estimated 6 percent of the population at that time—gave themselves voting rights under the original Constitution. As a society, we've since eliminated legal prohibitions on voting by African Americans, low-income people (who couldn't afford poll taxes), and women. But individuals with felony convictions are still mostly excluded from the ballot booth. In some states, their banishment lingers even after serving their sentences. The nation has seen an exponential surge in the number of incarcerations since the early 1970s, from about 330,000 in 1972 to 2.3 million today, making this category of disenfranchised individuals a significant one.

As with most voter laws, whether people with felony convictions can vote varies by state. As of 2019, forty-eight states prevent those serving their sentence (i.e., sitting in jail) from voting. What varies is the extent to which people who have completed their sentence, including probation and parole (and paid fines and fees), can vote.[10] In the majority of the forty-eight states, people on probation or parole also can't vote.

Somewhat remarkably, prisoners in the midst of serving their sentences in Maine and Vermont *can* vote. No other states have that blanket rule, although in some states, such as Maryland, people who are incarcerated for misdemeanors (e.g., failure to pay parking tickets, etc.) can vote from jail. This issue gets to the unique problem that many low-income people have in making cash bail—a problem that people of means do not face even if they are arrested for the same infraction.[11] In three states (Iowa, Kentucky, and Virginia), absent action from the governor, people with felony convictions lose their voting rights permanently, even if they never went to prison.

All told, author Mark Mauer reports that "an estimated 5.3 million persons are ineligible to vote as a result of a current or previous felony conviction" today. For complex reasons, these laws have a disproportionate impact on African Americans, in keeping with an ugly history of states "imposing disenfranchisement for crimes believed to be committed by blacks, but not so for crimes perceived to be engaged in by whites."[12] Some people with a felony conviction may not vote because they mistakenly believe they can't vote in their particular state.

To clear up a bit of that confusion, the appendix (pages 256 to 271) has a state-by-state chart on whether people with a felony record can vote.

You might be thinking at this point in the discussion, *Wait a minute. I am a citizen. I have a permanent residence, I am not homeless, and I have no felony record. Should I keep reading or skip to the next part?*

Hang on.

Throughout American history, those in power—both Democrats and Republicans—have sought to use voting laws as a way of preserving power by making it easier for their supporters to vote and/or making it harder for their political opponents to vote. The effects of large-scale disenfranchisement matter for who gets into office and what policies elected officials end up implementing while in office. Small margins of nonvoters can have a major impact on electoral outcomes. Keep in mind that President George W. Bush won the 2000 election by fewer than 600 Florida votes. Democratic incumbent Bill Nelson would likely have won the Florida Senate race over Republican Rick Scott in 2018 if people with felony records could have voted that year (Scott won by 10,033 votes). In 2010, Democrat Sarah Buxton won a seat in the Vermont House of Delegates by a single vote. In 2016, the same matchup was decided again by a single vote—but this time in favor of Republican David Ainsworth. And President Donald J. Trump won the swing state of Michigan by 11,837 votes—about the same number of people that fit into the University of Michigan's football stadium in Ann Arbor.[13]

As we've seen, voting rights in the United States are—somewhat surprisingly—not universal. They vary depending on where you live, and how you've lived. One thing remains constant, however: the ability to vote on who gets the people's power is absolutely fundamental to our democracy. Exercise it.

DISCUSSION QUESTIONS FOR CHAPTER 5

- Whether you agree with them or not, what might be the rationales for keeping noncitizens, the homeless, and/or people convicted of felonies away from the ballot box?

- On the other side of the scale, what are the rationales for embracing the right to vote for each of these categories of individuals?

- If you completed this little exercise, did it change your point of view about any aspect of this particular discussion? If yes, good for you. It's never a bad thing to challenge yourself to change your mind once in a while.

6

Key Ingredients to Electing a President (and What's the Electoral College, Anyway?)

Chapter 6 Takeaway Box

- We don't actually vote for the president in this country. We vote for "electors" whom we know nothing about.

- Whether your state's primary is open or closed makes a big difference in how much power the two major political parties have.
- In closed primary states, registering with a political party enhances your voting power.

This chapter discusses presidential elections. It covers how candidates get on the ballot, what it means to have a primary (and how it's different from a caucus), how the Electoral College works, and how the numbers for picking a president actually shake out. (Hint: Only a handful of states make a real difference in the Electoral College, a fact that creates all sorts of problems for American democracy, including cynicism about voting in the first place.)

Eligibility and Getting on the Ballot

The Constitution contains a handful of criteria for electing presidents. Article II, Section 1 provides that only a "natural born Citizen, or a Citizen of the United States" can be president. These terms are generally considered to mean that a person must be a citizen at the time of birth in order to be eligible for the presidency.[1] A presidential candidate must also "have attained to the Age of thirty five Years, and been fourteen Years a Resident within the United States." The Twelfth Amendment to the Constitution imposes the same requirements on vice presidents. (Senators need only be thirty years old, and members of the House of Representatives only twenty-five.)

To run for president, you also have to get on the presidential ballot. You do this by, first, completing a form—called "Form 2"—with the federal agency that oversees federal elections, the Federal Election Commission (FEC). This gets you on an FEC list called "Presidential Form 2 Filers."[2] Next, if you want to be a serious contender with your name listed alongside Bernie Sanders or Joe Biden, you need to get on the actual *state* ballots. This is hard to do. States have different requirements and deadlines. Major party candidates can be formally nominated at a national nominating convention, but that happens late in the game (more on this later). A majority of states (but not all) allow write-in candidates. But of course, if you are an unknown candidate, having your friends and family try to add you to the ballot isn't going to get you elected president.

If you run as an independent candidate, two states (Colorado and Louisiana) currently allow candidates to simply submit a filing fee and get on the ballot. But for the other forty-eight states plus the District of Columbia, you have to file a petition—which requires lots of signatures. For the 2016 election, an independent presidential candidate needed an estimated 860,000 signatures to run for president. Getting signatures requires candidates to amass campaign staff and volunteers in each state—and thus lots of money—before the race has even begun.[3] By default, only a tiny sliver of the American populace has a shot at becoming serious presidential contenders despite the broad eligibility criteria under the Constitution.

Caucuses versus Primaries

In general, only candidates from the two major parties—Republicans and Democrats—get automatic access to state ballots. The parties pick what names go on them. To add an entirely new party to the ballot, state laws require—you guessed it—that you file a petition containing lots of voters' names. For example, Virginia requires that a new party get 10 percent of the vote in a statewide race in one of the last two elections in order to get on a ballot. As we will discuss later, the two-party system in America has many problems. Ballot access laws are one of them, because they make it hard for new political parties with new ideas to gain traction.[4]

Strong third-party candidates are more likely to affect the outcome of the race between Democrats and the Republicans than to win the actual presidency. In 2000, for example, Green Party candidate Ralph Nader received 92,488 votes in Florida. The Florida vote tally decided a hotly disputed presidential election in favor of George W. Bush over Al Gore by a tiny margin of 537 votes. Without a doubt, Nader's inclusion in the race had a substantial impact.[5]

To winnow down the list of major party nominees, states hold what are called **primaries** or **caucuses** in the lead-up to the election. These processes allow voters to make their preferences known as to which candidate they want to be their party's official nominee for president. Most states hold primaries rather than caucuses. The process is spread out over five months, plus months of debates.

Primaries look like general elections in that people go to their polling places and vote for particular candidates in private. Primaries come in two forms: **open** and **closed**. In general, open primaries mean that anybody can participate—including independent voters, unaffiliated voters, or voters belonging to the other party. In some open primaries, voters select one party's ballot and pick from that list of candidates. So a Democrat could pick the Republican ballot and vice versa.

At one point, California had a system whereby all candidates from all parties were listed on the ballot, and voters could pick whom they liked even if it meant crossing party lines. The people with the most votes went to the general election. In 2000, the Supreme Court struck down California's law as unconstitutional under the First Amendment, on the rationale that it forced political parties to "associate with" individuals from other parties in the general election. The dissenting justices argued that the state had a sufficient justification for upholding the law: it expanded voters' participation in the electoral process. Whether you agree with the majority or dissent in this case depends in part on how much party loyalty—and the ability to pick your own party's nominee without influence from voters from another political party—means to you.[6]

In closed primaries, only registered party voters can vote for that party's candidates. Only registered Democrats can vote for Democratic nominees and only registered Republicans can vote for Republican nominees. Closed primaries are often criticized as enhancing the power of political parties over the preferences of individual voters. These days, many young people register as independents (instead of aligning with any one political party) and are shut out of the nominating process in closed primaries as a result. They can't vote for any primary candidates because they aren't registered with either the Democratic or Republican parties. Closed primaries also keep moderate voters who are registered with one party from voting for moderate candidates from another party.[7] Bottom line: if you want to maximize your voice in elections and you live in a closed primary state, you should register first with a major political party.

Primaries can also be either **direct** or **indirect**. In direct primaries, voters pick the party's nominee for president. In states with indirect primaries (as with caucuses, which we will cover in a moment), voters cast their ballots for a particular candidate but those votes don't go directly to the candidate. The votes instead go to delegates to the party's national convention who, in turn, are expected to cast their votes for the party's nominee in a manner consistent with voters' preference. (This process is similar to the Electoral College system, which we will get to later.)

So imagine you cast a vote for Jamal, who is running against Jane, for the Democratic Party nomination in your state. In some states, if Jamal wins the majority of the votes, he will automatically be the party's nominee for voters in that state. In other states, if Jamal wins the majority of the votes, he wins the delegates to the Democratic Convention. Those delegates are expected to vote for Jamal at the convention because that's what the voters' preference showed. (In some states, there are penalties if delegates vote in defiance of the voters, which rarely happens.)

Caucuses pick delegates rather than candidates—that is, they decide which representatives will go to the party's convention and cast a vote for a particular candidate. Instead of going to the polls, voters in caucus states who are registered with a particular party get together in a common meeting place. (The term "caucus" is said to come from the Algonquin term meaning "gathering of tribal chiefs.")[8] The party leaders go over core business at caucuses. Then caucus party attendees either gather into groups around a particular candidate or cast votes at the meeting (typically by secret ballot) for their preferred candidate, depending on the state and the party. Oftentimes, voters discuss the various candidates first and urge their friends to join their group or candidate. The numbers of voters favoring a particular candidate determines which delegates go to which candidates. The delegates, again, are then expected to cast their votes for president according to the caucus's vote. Although the vote-counting process for caucuses is not entirely accurate, major news outlets will declare the caucus "winners" as being those candidates with the highest percentage of delegates after a caucus. (For Democrats, this process was confused and delayed after the Iowa caucuses in 2020 due to technological glitches.)[9]

Party Nominations

The summer before each presidential election—which occurs every four years on the first Tuesday of November—each of the two major political parties holds a party convention. This has been going on since 1832, when the first convention occurred with the nomination of Andrew Jackson.[10] At a party convention, the party selects a nominee for president based on the number of votes cast by the party delegates at the convention. (Note that these people are delegates to the party's convention for purposes of picking a party *nominee* for president, not the president herself.) Conventions also establish party "platforms"—that is, the delegates agree upon a party's primary goals and its position on topics or issues of importance to the voters, such as taxes, immigration, or abortion access.

Each party has rules for choosing its own delegates. In the 2016 presidential election cycle, there were 2,472 delegates at the Republican Convention and 4,765 delegates at the Democratic Convention. For Democrats, presidential candidates get to propose potential delegates. In states with primaries, Democratic voters then choose the actual delegates at the ballot box. In states with caucuses, delegates are selected at state conventions that occur prior to the national convention. The Democratic Party awards delegates in proportion to the percentage of votes a candidate receives during the primaries and caucuses, as long as they receive at least 15 percent of the total votes (a number that makes them "viable"). So, for example, if Joe Schmendrick gets 50 percent of the vote in a particular district, he gets 50 percent of the delegates allotted to that district.

For Republican candidates, many states use a "winner-takes-all" method for awarding delegates. The candidate who gets the highest percentage of the votes in a district gets all the delegates for that district.

In our hypothetical, then, Joe would get all the state's delegates even though he only won 50 percent of the vote. Republican candidates can select (rather than merely propose) a quarter of their party's delegates. According to one Republican operative, the rest are chosen "by state conventions or executive committees consisting of local activists, volunteers and elected officials."[11]

Most convention delegates mechanically cast their votes according to the primary or caucus results—even if no law requires them to. Delegates who are not pledged to vote for a particular candidate are called "superdelegates," who first appeared in the 1980s. (They are not to be confused with "faithless electors" to the Electoral College, which we'll discuss shortly.) Superdelegates generally include members of Congress, governors, and—for the Democratic Party—members of the Democratic National Committee (DNC). The modern party convention is largely ceremonial, as each party's presumptive nominee is usually clear to the public long before the conventions take place. In theory, if no candidate wins a majority of delegates through the primaries and caucuses, a "brokered convention" could occur to resolve conflicts within the party. That hasn't happened since 1952, when Democrats wound up voting three separate times in order to nominate Adlai Stevenson at the convention. He later lost the presidential race to Dwight D. Eisenhower.[12]

The Electoral College

In 2018, there were nearly 111 million registered voters.[13] But in the United States, we don't just count up all the votes for president and decide who the winner is. Instead, we use what's called the Electoral College. We use the Electoral College because it's required by the Constitution. The Electoral College is not an institution of higher learning. It's a process. Under that process, a small group of people—538, to be exact—are designated to elect the president and vice president of the United States every four years. Each state gets the same number of people in the Electoral College as it has members of Congress. Under the Twenty-Third Amendment to the Constitution, the District of Columbia gets three electors.

To be elected president, a candidate needs 270 electoral votes. The total percentage of votes that go to one candidate or another across the US population—the so-called popular vote—is irrelevant to who wins the presidency. In other words, when you go to the polls to vote for president, you are actually voting for a subset of people within the 538 members of the Electoral College, not for the president or vice president directly. Each elector is supposed to cast his or her ballot for president and ballot for vice president according to the individual votes cast in that state. Most of the time, members of the Electoral College vote as they are supposed to—with rare exceptions. (The US Supreme Court is considering this issue in 2020.) In the controversial 2016 election, seven electors defected on the presidential ballot and six on the vice presidential ballot. But historically, such so-called faithless electors have not made the difference in terms of who won the office of the presidency.[14]

One of the reasons the framers of the Constitution installed the Electoral College was to ensure that candidates did not confine their campaigning to states with a lot of people. Today, some states are considered "competitive." The others are considered "safe states." Here's how many electoral votes each state gets as of this book's publication date (things might change after the 2020 census):[15]

STATE	NUMBER OF ELECTORAL VOTES
Alabama	9
Alaska	3
Arizona	11

STATE	NUMBER OF ELECTORAL VOTES
Arkansas	6
California	55
Colorado	9

STATE	NUMBER OF ELECTORAL VOTES
Connecticut	7
Delaware	3
District of Columbia	3
*Florida	29
Georgia	16
Hawaii	4
Idaho	4
Illinois	20
Indiana	11
Iowa	6
Kansas	6
Kentucky	8
Louisiana	8
Maine	4
Maryland	10
Massachusetts	11
*Michigan	16
Minnesota	10
Mississippi	6
Missouri	10
Montana	3
Nebraska	5
*Nevada	6

STATE	NUMBER OF ELECTORAL VOTES
*New Hampshire	4
New Jersey	14
New Mexico	5
New York	29
North Carolina	15
North Dakota	3
Ohio	18
Oklahoma	7
Oregon	7
*Pennsylvania	20
Rhode Island	4
South Carolina	9
South Dakota	3
Tennessee	11
Texas	38
Utah	6
Vermont	3
Virginia	13
Washington	12
West Virginia	5
*Wisconsin	10
Wyoming	3

*2020 core battleground states.

Total Electoral Votes: 538; Majority Needed to Elect: 270

As you can see, California, Texas, and New York have the most electoral votes for president, but they are not states with historically close races that could be won by either party—known as "swing states." People differ on what states will be battleground states in a particular election, but it's pretty safe to predict that California and New York will go to a Democrat. Few politicians prioritize campaigning in those states. While it might not "go blue" this cycle, Texas is "purpling" these days so both parties and candidates will be spending time and money there.

Which states hold the golden geese of electoral victory? Well, in the 2016 presidential election, eleven states were in play: Colorado, Florida, Iowa, Michigan, Nevada, New Hampshire, North Carolina, Ohio, Pennsylvania, Virginia, and Wisconsin. Some experts believe that Arizona and Georgia might also be "swingy" in 2020, but many agree that the core battleground states will include Florida, Michigan, Nevada, New Hampshire, Pennsylvania, and Wisconsin.[16] (They're marked with an asterisk in the chart so you know a bit more about which electoral votes will likely matter for 2020.) Note that Florida voters decided in 2018 to give most convicted felons the right to vote, which could dramatically swing elections in Democrats' favor. In response, Florida politicians have tacked on laws requiring payment of all court-related fees and fines in advance of voting, which—depending on the outcome of litigation challenging those laws—could effectively leave some people with prior felony records out in the cold on Election Day in 2020.[17]

If our vote for president isn't actually a vote for a presidential nominee but a vote for one or more electors, how are electors chosen? After all, their names don't normally appear on the actual ballots we see on Election Day. The Constitution only says that members of Congress can't be electors. Nor can any "Person holding an Office of Trust or Profit under the United States" (a phrase that is undefined). Under the Fourteenth Amendment—a post–Civil War reform—state officials who engaged in insurrection or rebellion against the United States cannot serve in the Electoral College either.[18]

Beyond that, states get to decide the procedures that apply for selecting electors. Each state's political parties choose potential electors prior to the presidential election. In general, the two primary political parties nominate slates of possible electors at their state party conventions. Alternatively, the parties' central committees vote on who should be that party's electors for that state in a given presidential election year. The state or national party decides on the rules for making those selections. It should come as no surprise that electors are often chosen based on their loyalty and service to that political party. They could be state legislators, party leaders, or donors. If you want to know how your electors are chosen, you have to ask your state or local party officials for the rules. If this sounds to you like an insider's game, you're right. If it sounds oddly anti-democratic, you're right again. A meaningful vote arguably assumes—at a minimum—that the voter knows whom they are voting for and why that person is an elector in the first place. But that's not how it works in America.[19]

Although the media "calls" the presidential election on Election Day, the actual election of the president and vice president takes place through the Electoral College over a month later. The electors cast their votes in the state's capital on the first Monday after the second Wednesday in December, which in 2016 fell on the nineteenth. In a joint session of Congress on January 6 at 1:00 P.M., the vice president formally presides over the vote count and the results are officially announced, with the vice president declaring the next president. (Recall that Vice President Al Gore famously executed this duty with dignity and decorum after the Supreme Court refused to allow a recount to go forward in the disputed Florida election for president in 2000.)[20]

Keep in mind, however, that states get to set their own rules for elections under the Constitution. Not all Electoral College votes are cast in the same way. The US Supreme Court has declared that "the appointment and mode of appointment of electors belong[s] exclusively to the states under the Constitution of the United States."[21] In most states and in the District of Columbia, the candidate who gets most of that state's popular votes gets *all* of that state's Electoral College ballots. In only two states—Maine and Nebraska—are the Electoral College votes cast according to the percentage of votes cast for particular candidates in individual congressional districts.

Maryland, for example, is divided into eight congressional districts, each of which sends its own member to the US House of Representatives. (Recall that each state gets two senators, regardless of its relative size and population.) If Joe gets 50.1 percent of the popular vote in Maryland and Jane gets 49.9 percent, Joe will still get *all* eight of the Electoral College votes. If Maryland instead allocated its Electoral College votes by the electoral outcomes in each congressional district (like Maine and Nebraska do), Joe might only get four or five Electoral College votes while Jane might get three or four. This distinction between a winner-takes-all and a proportional allocation of electors is an important one. George W. Bush won the presidential election in 2000 by 271 Electoral College votes—only one vote over the 270-vote margin needed to win. In 2004, he won by a mere fifteen votes in the Electoral College. If some of the winner-takes-all states instead allocated electors according to the proportion of votes favoring one candidate over the other, Al Gore would have won additional electors in the 2000 race. With only two more electors in his column, Gore would have won the presidency, shifting the course of history. (He did win the popular vote, after all.)

The 2000 election is not the only time that the Electoral College handed the presidency to a candidate who lost the popular vote. It has happened four more times in the nation's history, most recently in 2016, when Donald J. Trump won the Electoral College—and thus the presidency—but lost the popular vote to Hillary Clinton. (Andrew Jackson also lost to John Quincy Adams in 1824, Samuel Tilden lost to Rutherford B. Hayes in 1876, and Grover Cleveland lost to Benjamin Harrison in 1888.) In fact, if a presidential candidate only wins the eleven states with the most electoral votes, she will hit 270 and win the presidency—regardless of whether people in the remaining thirty-nine states and the District of Columbia voted for her.[22]

How did America wind up with this bizarre Electoral College process? The answer is in Article II of the original US Constitution. It provided that each member of the Electoral College gets to vote for two people, either of whom could wind up being president. The person getting the most votes won the presidency, and the runner-up became the vice president. (This was kind of like an early version of "ranked choice voting," which we'll cover later in the book; it's making a comeback in some state and local elections.)

This system presented problems in the 1800 presidential election, because Thomas Jefferson and Aaron Burr each won seventy-three electoral votes, creating a tie. The Constitution tasked the outgoing House of Representatives with holding a second election to choose between Jefferson and Burr. Although Jefferson won that runoff election in Congress, the debacle led to passage of the Twelfth Amendment, which was ratified in 1804, and still applies today. Under the Twelfth Amendment, members of the Electoral College vote separately for president and vice president to avoid tie votes. (The other constitutional change to presidential elections since ratification of the original Constitution appears in the Twenty-Second Amendment, which confined the presidency to two terms—or a total of eight years—in office.)

As a practical matter, the Electoral College means that some electors' votes—and thus the views of the individual voters they represent—don't matter much to presidential candidates. To be sure, demographics shift. But traditionally, states like California, New York, and the District of Columbia have gone to Democrats. States like Texas, Wyoming, and Georgia have traditionally gone to Republicans (although Texas and possibly Georgia are currently in flux). Florida and Ohio have generally been considered "swing" or "battleground" states because they have lots of Electoral College votes, which neither party can take for granted (although Ohio is considered comfortably Republican these days). As a result, more campaign dollars—and candidates' attention—go to states that are toss-ups than to the ones that are shoo-ins.[23] If you are a Democrat in Oklahoma or a Republican in California and you want your vote for president to count, you'd better pick up and move to a swing state. Of course, your vote for all the other "down-ballot" races still counts!

Calls for scrapping the Electoral College are real. According to a POLITICO/Morning Consult poll of registered voters in March 2019, 50 percent believed that a national popular vote should decide presidential elections. Only 34 percent favored the Electoral College system. Overall, Democrats and independents showed more support for the popular vote than did Republicans.[24] But changing the system is hard to do. It would require a constitutional amendment, which is nearly impossible to accomplish. A constitutional amendment requires the bipartisan support of two-thirds of the US House of Representatives and two-thirds of the Senate, as well as ratification by three-quarters of the states. These days, Congress can't seem to achieve a bipartisan anything anymore.

A handful of states are trying to get around the amendment process by signing onto something called the "National Popular Vote Interstate Compact." It's an agreement among certain states that their electoral votes will go to the candidate who wins the popular vote, regardless of how each member state's population actually votes. If the pact were in place and President Trump were to win the popular vote in 2020, for example, all fifty-five of California's delegates to the Electoral College would go to Trump—even if California voters overall choose the Democratic candidate. The pact only kicks in if states with a combined total of 270 or more electoral votes join the agreement. In battleground states, the pact would mean fewer political dollars coming in during presidential elections, so the measure is controversial for this reason (and a number of others). Candidates would have to compete across the nation for votes instead of focusing all their efforts in the swing states. As of March 2019, eighty-one more electoral votes are needed for the pact to reach its 270 vote threshold. An additional fifteen states have introduced legislation in favor of it. (Whether the agreement could be enforced by noncompliant state officials in the midst of a heated election is an entirely different matter.)[25]

Given today's substantial public support for abolishing the Electoral College, why did the Constitution's framers create it in the first place? In the words of Yale Law School professor Akhil Reed Amar, "[i]t is often said that the Founders chose the electoral college over direct election in order to balance the interests of big (high-population) and small (low-population) states." If this was the true rationale, it didn't exactly pan out. Although smaller rural states lean Republican, some large states with a lot of electoral votes—like California (55) and New York (29)—tend to go with Democrats, including the 2016 nominee, Hillary Clinton, who lost the 2016 election despite winning the popular vote. Texas (38), Florida (29), and Pennsylvania (20) historically favor Republicans.

Another rationale for the Electoral College raised by Professor Amar is that "[o]rdinary Americans across a vast continent would lack sufficient information to choose intelligently among leading presidential candidates." Of course, when the Constitution took effect in 1798, only white male landowners could vote. All women as well as men of color were banned from the ballot box. Life in the eighteenth century was highly provincial. The Constitution's drafters were understandably concerned that voters would lack sufficient information to cast informed ballots about presidential candidates from out of state. Professor Amar adds, however, that "[t]he early emergence of national presidential parties rendered the objection obsolete . . . by linking presidential candidates to slates of local candidates and national platforms that explained to voters who stood for what."[26] The rationale may be more obsolete today because we are bombarded with round-the-clock global information overload through the internet, smartphones, and social media, although some of it is full of inaccuracies.

Amar gives another, especially problematic rationale for the Electoral College: slavery. At the constitutional convention in Philadelphia in 1787, a proposal was made for directly electing the president—that is, all nationwide votes are tallied and the person with the most votes wins. James Madison responded that the system would be problematic for the South, whose 500,000 slaves could not vote: "The right of suffrage was much more diffusive [i.e., extensive] in the Northern than the Southern States," he said, "and the latter could have no influence in the election on the score of the Negroes." Because the composition of the Electoral College is ultimately based on each state's population—not on the numbers of registered voters in each state—the nonvoting slave population in the South did not negatively affect those states' influence in presidential elections. By the same token, the Electoral College created little incentive for states to extend the right to vote to formerly enslaved men or to women.[27]

These justifications carry no weight today. A key argument favoring retention of the Electoral College instead goes like this: A direct election could invite lots of additional candidates. In that event, nobody would win a majority of the votes. Instead, the process would produce winners of a plurality of votes—in a four-way race, for example, the winner might get 28 percent of the vote, with the other candidates gleaning 24 percent or less each. Imagine a multitude of parties—say, pro-life and pro-choice parties, climate change and anti-regulation parties, pro-immigration and anti-immigration parties, and so on—and then imagine a splintered vote among them, with the candidate who wins the largest percentage of votes declared the winner. Without buy-in from a substantial segment of the American people, a presidential winner would not have the necessary mandate to govern effectively.

A numerical cutoff could be imposed to address the plurality problem—requiring, let's say, 45 percent of the vote to win the presidency. But then elections would drag on and on with runoff elections required to choose between candidates who didn't get 45 percent of the vote. But this concern may be overblown. Many states already elect governors with plurality votes, yet that hasn't ground gubernatorial elections to a virtual halt. Moreover, the system could be designed such that voters rank their favorite candidates on the ballot. And as we've discussed, procedures already exist for limiting the ability of new political parties to get on the presidential ballot.[28]

There's no getting around the fact that the Electoral College is a problem for anyone who believes that every individual's vote counts—regardless of where you live. Presidential candidates should care about persuading the majority of the American electorate, not just those who happen to live in battleground states. But even if you live in a solidly blue or red state, it's imperative that you engage in your constitutional ability to participate in self-governance and vote. If it becomes a habit, your votes in local, state, and national elections *will* matter over the course of a lifetime. And taking the time to vote shows respect for the great privilege of being able to participate in free elections—something that millions of people across the globe can only dream about.

To see how your state fares in the Electoral College, take a look at this map, which lists the number of electors per state:

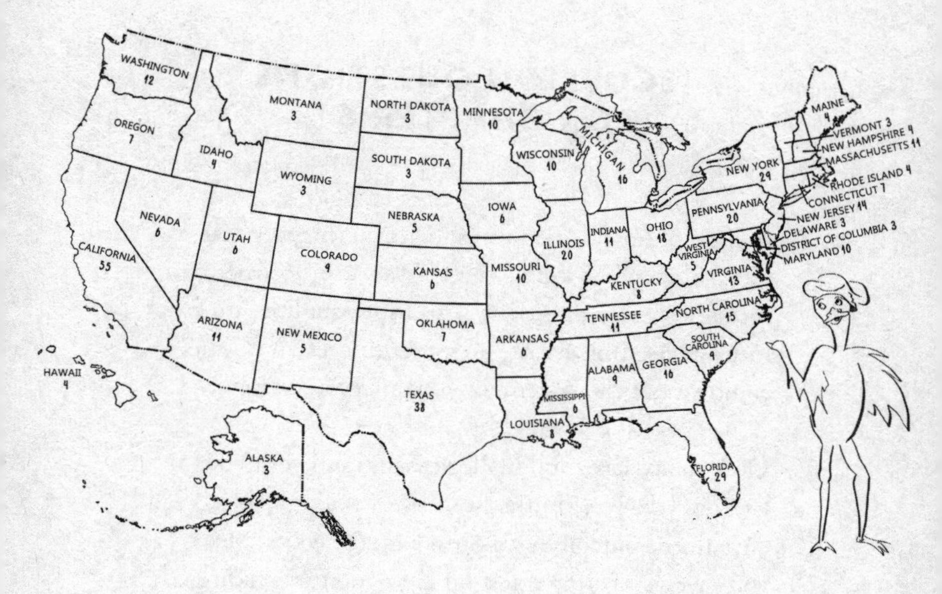

For 2020, pollsters predict that the keys to victory for either party could be Wisconsin, Michigan, and Pennsylvania. Trump lost the popular vote by nearly three million votes, and winning the electoral votes from these three states would have put Hillary Clinton in the White House. Together, they carry forty-six electoral votes, representing 34.4 million people out of a total US population of 327 million. Fewer than 34.4 million people in these states—let's guesstimate half, or 17.2 million—are registered voters, and even fewer of these actually vote. How comfortable are you with a sliver of the population effectively deciding the next presidential election? If the answer is "not very," then we agree that it's time to pay attention to the right to vote in America.

DISCUSSION QUESTIONS FOR CHAPTER 6

- In light of how difficult it is to get on the presidential ballot, what kinds of qualities are needed to actually run for president? Are those qualities uniformly based on merit, or something else? If you could tweak the system, how would you tweak it?

- How many Electoral College votes does your state get, and do you think those votes make a difference in the outcome of a presidential election? Did your views on this question change after reading this chapter? Why or why not?

- Every election year, we hear how important segments of the American public want real change in Washington, DC. How feasible is such change so long as we have a two-party system in America, which is prescribed nowhere in the Constitution?

7

Key Ingredients to Electing People to Congress

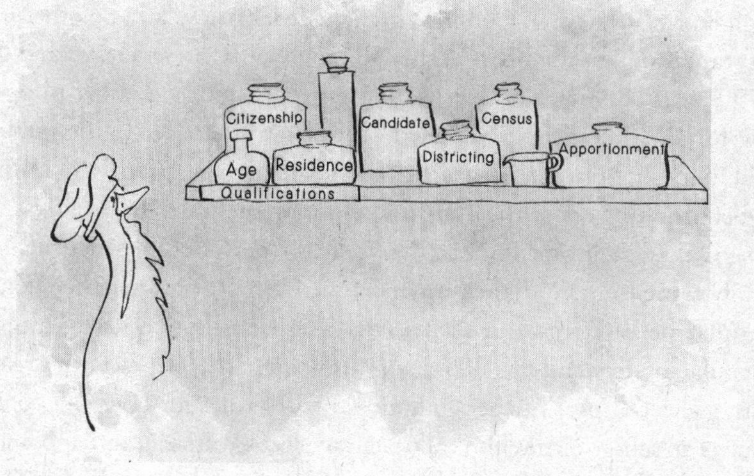

Chapter 7 Takeaway Box

- The number of House of Representatives members your state gets depends on the census and how many people (not citizens, mind you) live there.
- Every state gets two senators, regardless of population.

- When a member of Congress dies in office, you might have nobody representing you for a while (as is always the case for residents of Washington, DC). Is that a concern?

This chapter discusses congressional elections—how voters choose who will represent them in Congress to make federal laws and do other important things as members of the US House of Representatives and the US Senate. Remember that the US government is designed to operate for "We the People." Elected officials are there to do the public's bidding—not use that power to benefit themselves. Bear this in mind when thinking about the duties of your representatives in Congress.

Unlike the British monarchy, where the power of the ruler theoretically came from God, the framers of the US Constitution emboldened regular people to govern themselves. The Constitution itself—unlike popular understandings of a deity—is not a *source* of power. It's really just a sheet of parchment containing a set of rules for how *the people*'s power to self-govern will be allocated to elected officials and appointed judges. Ultimately, the people remain in charge, at least in theory. They do this by casting ballots in federal elections. If they don't enforce the piece of paper at the ballot box—meaning if they don't enforce consequences for bad behavior by elected officials—then the Constitution will become meaningless and power will increasingly be abused. A piece of paper has no power on its own.

We already talked about elections for president. Electing people to Congress is no less important, because Congress does a number of things, including making laws that bind the conduct of the rest of us. Congress also is tasked with keeping the executive and judicial branches in check. And unlike presidents, members of Congress can serve for life (so long as they are reelected, of course). They have no term limits. Because Congress is bipartisan, with members from both sides of the political aisle (plus an independent or two), it's in a different political posture than a president, who hails exclusively from one of the two major parties and generally populates her cabinet with like-minded appointees. Bipartisanship in Congress can be a beautiful thing for democracy and "We the People," although it's bordering on extinction these days.

House of Representatives

As we know, the legislative branch of the federal government has two parts: the House of Representatives and the Senate. Under Article I, Section 2 of the Constitution, voters pick members of the House of Representatives every two years in popular elections. The two-year window impacts how things are done in the House and, in theory at least, keeps members tied to the needs and concerns of their constituencies: the voters. Who sits in the House of Representatives might change after each election. As a consequence, policy initiatives—that is, ideas for new laws that may be popular or unpopular among American voters—may die when new people come on board every two years.

The Constitution requires that members of the House of Representatives be twenty-five years old and citizens of the United States for at least seven years when they're elected to office. They also have to physically live in the state that they are elected to represent. As of 2020, most members of the House of Representatives make $174,000 per year. Majority and minority leaders receive more—$193,400—and the House Speaker gets $223,500.[1] The same range of paychecks generally goes to senators.

The Constitution says a few more things about picking members of the House of Representatives. As noted earlier in the book, it gives the *states* control over "The Times, Places, and Manner of holding Elections for Senators and Representatives." States make election rules in their legislatures (remember that each state has its own three-branch system of government, which includes governors and courts too). All fifty states have their own prerequisites for people who want to run for the House of Representatives, such as filing fees or petitions containing a minimum number of signatures. The Constitution allows Congress to change most of the states' election laws if it wants to, however. This is important to keep in mind in thinking about entrenched problems with the processes for electing presidents and members of Congress, which we will get to later in the book.

The Constitution also provides that each state gets at least one representative in the House, but it says that the total number of representatives per state can't be more than one elected official for every thirty thousand people in the state. Translated, this means that the number of representatives each state gets in the House will depend on each state's population. The Constitution provides for a federal census—which it calls an "Enumeration"—every ten years. It also states that "Representatives and direct Taxes shall be apportioned among the several States which may be included within this Union, according to their respective Numbers."[2]

The Impact of the Census

The word *apportioned* is a biggie here. Census numbers determine how many representatives each state gets in the House of Representatives, and how much of certain categories of federal funding goes to each state. The higher the number of actual heads in a state, the more representation and money that state gets. The fewer people counted, the fewer people who go to the House of Representatives for that state and the fewer federal dollars that go to address the needs of the people living in that state.

In 2019, the US Supreme Court held in a 5–4 decision called *Department of Commerce v. New York* that the Trump administration could not add a question about citizenship to the 2020 census form. This decision received a lot of press, and for good reason. The Trump administration lost the case because the evidence showed that the reason that Department of Commerce secretary Wilbur Ross gave for asking people on the 2020 census whether they're US citizens was a manufactured one. Ross claimed that the question was necessary to assist the government in enforcing the Voting Rights Act (VRA). But as Chief Justice Roberts noted, Ross wanted to add the question "about a week into his tenure" when there was "no hint that he was considering VRA enforcement in connection with that project." In fact, a top staffer "did not know why the secretary wished to reinstate the question, but saw it as his task to 'find the best rationale.'"

To that end, Ross's team tried to get the Department of Homeland Security and the Department of Justice's Executive Office of Immigration Review to ask the Department of Commerce to add the question so that Ross could have a justification for including it. Those attempts failed. Ultimately, Ross contacted then–attorney general Jeff Sessions and got what he was looking for: DOJ's Civil Rights Division expressed interest in the citizenship data in order "to better enforce the VRA." But the Supreme Court majority ruled that "the VRA enforcement rationale—the sole stated reason [for adding the question]—seems to have been contrived." Because agencies must "offer genuine justifications for important decisions, reasons that can be scrutinized by courts and the interested public," the court sent the question back to the Commerce Department to try again, effectively in ten years.[3]

As a result of that decision, for the next decade noncitizens will continue to be counted in the census. That outcome is fine with the Constitution as it doesn't limit head-counting to citizens. The framers of the Constitution knew that in England, seats in Parliament were instead determined arbitrarily—some large towns had only one member, just like certain small boroughs. As law professor Garrett Epps explains: "The framers wanted the U.S. House of Representatives to be 'the people's house,' and to do that, distribution of seats had to be fair."[4]

The wide-ranging political ramifications of this recent Supreme Court decision are what make it controversial—not its legal basis. Evidence showed that many people who aren't citizens would have not fully answered the census for fear that they might be deported for admitting they are not citizens. According to Harvard University research, adding the citizenship question would have "significantly increase[d] the percent of questions skipped, with particularly strong effects among Hispanics," making "respondents less likely to report having members of their household who are of Hispanic ethnicity." When extrapolated to the general population, the research results also suggested "that asking about citizenship [would have] reduce[d] the number of Hispanics reported in the 2010 Census by approximately 4.2 million, or around 8.4 percent of the 2010 Hispanic population."[5]

There are still a lot of reasons to believe that people will be afraid to fill out the census for fear of deportation despite this Supreme Court decision—namely, certain government policies have led immigrant communities to hide from the government and stay away from social services even if they are legally entitled to them. This is unfortunate. If the government is to properly account for state populations, it's important that everyone fill out the census form fully and accurately.

The reason some people see the decision as a political blow is that Hispanics tend to vote Democratic. And they're one of the fastest-growing ethnic populations in the United States. The number of Hispanic voters in midterm elections grew "from 2.9 million in 1986 to 6.8 million in 2014," while "turnout—measured as a percentage of total eligible adults 18 and over—has experienced a relative decline," from 38.7 percent to 27.1 percent over the same time period. If the turnout rate had remained steady, it would have meant nearly two million more ballots cast by Hispanics in the 2014 midterms—a year in which Hispanic support for Democratic House candidates was 62 percent. By contrast, support for Republicans was 36 percent.[6]

In short, the Constitution is clear that census tallies must be used for apportionment of the House of Representatives, and for now those tallies will include noncitizens. But the actual method for dividing up representatives among the states based on those numbers is not laid out in the Constitution. In fact, the Constitution does not even state whether the number of representatives in the House should increase as overall population increases. (Interesting fact: according to the first census, the US population was 3.89 million in 1790. That census categorized people according to enslaved status, sex, and age, including free white males aged sixteen and older, younger free white males, free white females, all other free people, and slaves. By comparison, the US resident population was 308 million according to the 2010 census, a number that's grown by approximately 20 million since then.)[7]

Until the early twentieth century, the method Congress used to apportion representatives in the House wound up largely increasing—or at least preserving—most states' existing representation in that chamber. The original size of the House of Representatives was 65 members, rising to 435 after the 1910 census. Over time, some states wound up overrepresented—with too many people in the House of Representatives based on some states' relative populations—and others underrepresented. Following the 1920 census, Congress couldn't figure out a way to successfully conduct the census—even though the Constitution required to. In short, Congress couldn't manage to divide up the representatives in the House as it was supposed to do.

Congress responded in 1929 by passing a law capping the maximum number of people in the House of Representatives at 435—the level established after the 1910 census. This is still the law today. The 1929 law also set forth a mathematical formula for automatically reapportioning seats in the House of Representatives going forward. (Another interesting fact: the District of Columbia, Puerto Rico, and the four other island territories of the US—American Samoa, Guam, the Northern Mariana Islands, and the US Virgin Islands—do not have a voting member of the House of Representatives. They each send a delegate, but that person cannot vote. These territories have no representation in the Senate.)[8]

Some scholars argue that, because unfair representation is increasingly a problem, the 1929 law needs a rewrite. On average, each person in the House of Representatives represents around 750,000 people, based on current US population estimates. This leaves an individual's vote so diluted that it may not matter to elected members of the House of Representatives if any one person—or even groups of people—feels frustrated with the job they are doing. In Britain, that number is closer to 97,000 people per representative in the legislature. In Canada and France, it's 114,000. It's been estimated that if the size of the House had been increased from 435 to 500 prior to the 2000 election, Al Gore would have won the presidency over George W. Bush. Recall that under Article II, Section 1 of the Constitution, the number of electors a state has in the Electoral College equals the total number of representatives the state has in Congress, both House and Senate seats, so apportionment in the House matters for presidential elections too. In 2009, the statute fixing the House at 435 members was challenged in court as unconstitutional—without success. It remains the law of the land, even though the 435 number is not in the Constitution itself.[9]

Generally speaking, less populous states like Alaska and Delaware each send one person to the House of Representatives (despite how small their populations may be). More populous states—like California (53 members) and New York (27)—are carved up into legislative subdivisions called **districts**. Each district within a state sends one member of Congress to the House of Representatives. But how the states get carved up is highly political and controversial, as we'll discuss later.

As of 2020, here's how the various states fare in terms of the numbers of representatives each state has in the House:[10]

STATE	NUMBER OF REPRESENTATIVES
Alabama	7
Alaska	1
Arizona	9
Arkansas	4
California	53
Colorado	7
Connecticut	5
Delaware	1
Florida	27
Georgia	14
Hawaii	2
Idaho	2
Illinois	18
Indiana	9
Iowa	4
Kansas	4
Kentucky	6
Louisiana	6
Maine	2
Maryland	8
Massachusetts	9
Michigan	14
Minnesota	8
Mississippi	4
Missouri	8
Montana	1

STATE	NUMBER OF REPRESENTATIVES
Nebraska	3
Nevada	4
New Hampshire	2
New Jersey	12
New Mexico	3
New York	27
North Carolina	13
North Dakota	1
Ohio	16
Oklahoma	5
Oregon	5
Pennsylvania	18
Rhode Island	2
South Carolina	7
South Dakota	1
Tennessee	9
Texas	36
Utah	4
Vermont	1
Virginia	11
Washington	10
West Virginia	3
Wisconsin	8
Wyoming	1
TOTAL	435

Senate

Unlike for the House of Representatives, senators are elected by voters across the state—not district-by-district. At this point, state lines are virtually set in stone, and they don't change based on electoral redistricting.

Most voters know that they go to the ballot box and elect senators from time to time, just like they elect members of the House. But it wasn't always this way. Under Article I, Section 3 of the *original* Constitution, senators were chosen by the state legislatures. This is the way things were done until the mid-1850s, at which point state political parties became so hostile to each other that they couldn't elect any candidate to the Senate, leaving vacancies in that body. In 1866, Congress passed a law regulating how states were to elect senators, but problems persisted, including bribes, deadlocks, and empty Senate seats.

After decades of debate over whether senators should be chosen by direct elections rather than by representatives in state legislatures, the Seventeenth Amendment was sent to the states for ratification in 1912. The required three-fourths majority needed for enactment occurred in 1913. In 1914, senators were for the first time "elected by the people"—not "chosen by the Legislature" of each state.[11]

There are two other important differences between the election of senators and the election of members of the House of Representatives: the number of years senators serve and how many each state gets. On these issues, the original Constitution hasn't changed. Senators serve six-year terms. The six-year term of office means that one-third of the Senate's members must be reelected every two years. The elections are staggered so that only about a third of the Senate is up for reelection in any given year, which makes the Senate very hard to "flip" politically, so to speak. In addition, each state only gets two senators.

The age and citizenship requirements for senators are different than those for House members, as well. Senators must be thirty years old and have been US citizens for at least nine years. Thus, immigrants can become members of the House of Representatives and the Senate. (Another interesting fact: the framers of the Constitution figured that, without the residency requirement, senators could be susceptible to foreign influence, while a complete ban on immigrants serving in Congress would dampen immigration and offend European supporters of the Revolutionary War effort.)[12]

Article I, Section 3 of the Constitution also states that the vice president of the United States "shall be President of the Senate, but shall have no Vote unless they be equally divided." In other words, the vice president casts votes in the Senate only to break a tie. Otherwise, the Constitution states, "the Senate shall chuse their other Officers, and also a President pro tempore." The Senate president pro tempore is a sitting senator who breaks ties if the vice president is not available. The Senate has a secretary, a sergeant at arms, a doorkeeper, a chaplain, and other staff whose job it is to help things run smoothly. These people aren't elected.[13]

As of the 2018 midterm elections, Republicans controlled fifty-three seats in the Senate (reflecting a net gain of two seats), and Democrats controlled forty-five seats. The remaining two seats in the 116th Congress are held by independents in Maine and Vermont. These independent senators caucus—that is, they meet to pursue common legislative objectives—with Democrats.[14]

Special Elections

A special election occurs in Congress when a vacancy arises during a member's term for any reason, such as death or resignation to take another job. Vacancies in the House are not filled the same way as vacancies in the Senate and can take much longer.

Under Article I, Section 2 of the Constitution, "[w]hen vacancies happen in the Representation from any State, the Executive Authority thereof shall issue Writs of Election to fill such Vacancies." What this means is that the state's governor must call for an actual election to fill a vacant seat in the House of Representatives—she cannot simply appoint a temporary replacement. A special election requires a full election process, including nominations, a primary, and a general election in the congressional district involved. This cycle typically takes three to six months. While a seat is vacant, the people in that congressional district do not have a voting representative in the House. Instead, the former representative's staff keeps the office going and is supervised by the clerk of the House of Representatives. Constituents are left to press senators for policy initiatives until the seat is filled.

Unlike for the House, the Constitution doesn't have mandatory rules for filling Senate vacancies. Recall that the Seventeenth Amendment changed the way that senators are elected—instead of having state legislatures do it, the people now pick senators at the ballot box. The Seventeenth Amendment provides that Senate vacancies can be filled by special elections, as the Constitution requires for the House of Representatives. But it also allows governors to make temporary appointments. State legislatures get to decide which process applies—a special election or an appointment by the governor. Alaska, Oregon, and Wisconsin don't allow their governors to appoint senators to fill vacancies. For states that give governors that power, some require that he pick someone from the same political party as that of the outgoing senator. The appointee serves as a full-capacity senator until an election is held—usually that means a general election rather than a special election.[15]

When Arizona senator John McCain died in August 2018, for example, Arizona governor Doug Ducey appointed former US senator Jon Kyl to fill the vacancy. After Kyl resigned in December 2018, Ducey appointed Martha McSally to replace him. She will serve until either she—or another candidate—is chosen to fill the vacancy by a special election, which is slated for 2020. The special election winner will then serve until the general election takes place in 2022.[16]

Getting on the Congressional Ballot

This is a book about voting, which is the primary way that individual citizens affect their government. Another way to do that is to run for office. That can seem daunting at first blush, but lots of regular people are managing to do it these days. Some states have fees, others make you get a petition of signatures, and some do both. Some states also have special requirements for small parties and independent candidates. If you're someone who is curious about that path, there is another chart for you in the appendix on pages 272 to 301.

If you are not someone who wants to get as involved as running for a seat, you could simply get involved in the elections! Politicians are always looking for volunteers to help with their campaigns throughout the election. Use the charts in this book, including the one in the appendix on how to register, to find links to candidates. From there, reach out to the candidates you think you are interested in working with and see how you can help with their campaign. You could make a huge difference.

DISCUSSION QUESTIONS FOR CHAPTER 7

- Now that you have a primer on elections to the House of Representatives and the role of the census in deciding how many members each state sends to Congress, do you agree that 435 is a reasonable cap on the total number of people in the House?

- We will talk about problems with our electoral system later in the book, but did anything surprise or trouble you in reading this chapter? If so, why?

- How important is it that people vote in primaries these days? If we assume that it is hard to flip gerrymandered districts (more on that later), can voters from the opposite side of the political aisle get their voices heard by voting for more moderate candidates in primaries? If the answer is yes, do you have a new appreciation for open primaries?

PART III

Why Your Right to Vote Is in Danger Today

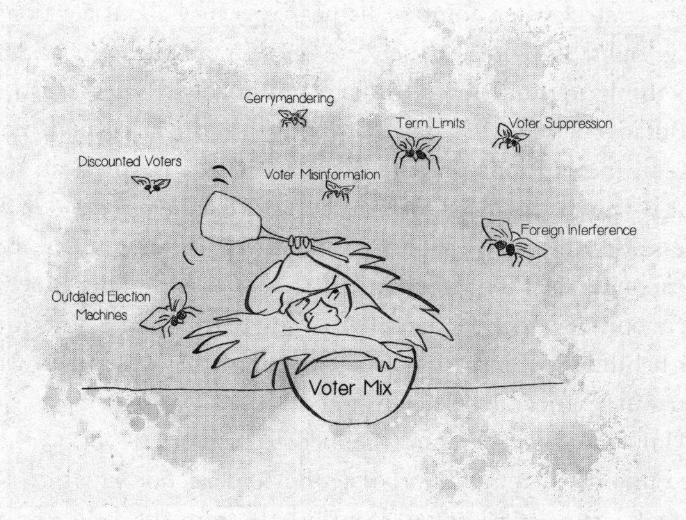

The concept behind the right to vote is pretty simple. Americans are not "subjects" to be ruled by a king, a queen, or a tyrannical megaboss. We aren't to be ruled at all. We rule ourselves. We pick our own bosses. We consent to our government. Government is supposed to work for "We the People"—not the other way around. If the government fails to do what we want it to do, it gets fired. No one person can do the firing. Absent impeachment in the Congress, "We the People" have to band together—in the thousands or millions—to fire a president and other government officials covered by the impeachment process.

Those who stay home from the polls essentially consent to be governed by whomever winds up in office. The link between an individual voter's life and the people in power is usually pretty weak. This reality makes caring about the theory behind voting hard. The notion that we are the boss of the president and Congress and the governor and mayor and our local school board members and on and on is pretty esoteric and abstract. "Click" goes the button on the TV remote control when some of us hear speeches about elections and voting, right? Oftentimes, there are much more engaging and glamorous things to think about, and our minds crave those instead.

But it's not a stretch to say that voting—and American democracy itself—is in peril today. That's not new news for American history. What is new is the influx of big data and technology on our voting process, as well as the established attempts by hostile foreign powers to weaponize the First Amendment against us and undermine public trust in our system of elections. It's not just entrenched politicians who work behind the scenes for power. Some foreign governments want to undermine democratic elections too.

Unfortunately, there are a bunch of barriers to voting that are baked into the system and pre-date the 2016 election in which Russia interfered. Such barriers can keep people from the polls and make their votes insignificant even if they manage to cast them. This is the case whether you believe voting is a privilege or a right. In other words, even if you believe that only certain additional categories of people are "rightful" voters, your vote might not count at the end of the day, anyway. Who, then, is in charge of our democracy? If it's not "We the People," who is it?

These are legitimate and ultimately unanswerable questions. There's no easy fix for the human desire to amass power and use it to one's own advantage—whether that user be a colleague or boss in the workplace, a domestic politician, a hostile foreign power, or a corporate CEO. The only answer to making sure that the government is accountable to the people and not able to bully our neighbors (and ultimately ourselves) is to make our will known, collectively, at the polls. That's so long as that ability still remains in America to a meaningful degree, which isn't a given, either. There are many reasons why.

The top issues concerning voting in America are these: gerrymandering, the lack of term limits in Congress, a Senate that by constitutional design weights certain votes more than others, a system that discounts voters who chose candidates that didn't get a majority or plurality of votes, corporate and "dark" money in politics, voter suppression, voter misinformation, and outdated election machines. Note that I'm not adding voter fraud to this list because there isn't any empirical data suggesting that it's a real problem in the way the others are. Still, it's the primary reason that politicians use to justify making voting categorically harder, so the issue needs to be understood. This last part of the book walks through each of these issues not to convince people of one point of view or another, but to increase awareness of these issues so that regular people can begin to think about them. (Politicians think about them already.) As for what to do about these intrinsic problems with voting in America, the answer isn't despair or complacency. The answer is to vote.

8

How Dug in Are Politicians? Gerrymandering and Limitless Terms for Congress

Chapter 8 Takeaway Box

- Gerrymandering is a serious threat to democracy because it allows politicians to manipulate the system in their favor.
- The Supreme Court has shut the door to

addressing partisan gerrymandering through the federal courts as a matter of constitutional law.

- Some people believe that term limits for Congress would make politicians more accountable to voters.

This chapter talks about two of the barriers to meaningful voting in America: gerrymandering and the lack of term limits in Congress. Gerrymandering lets politicians pick their voters—not the other way around. It means that certain congressional districts are unwinnable by Republican candidates and that certain congressional districts are unwinnable by Democratic candidates—no matter what the voters overall in those states want. Gerrymandering is about keeping certain political parties in power. It was in the public eye in 2019 because of a very important Supreme Court decision holding that the political process—not the courts—has to address the problem if it's addressed at all. Federal courts and the Constitution are categorically out of the picture.

The lack of congressional term limits sounds like a nothing-burger by comparison, because if voters want to reelect the same person to Congress over and over and over again, that's their prerogative, right? Well, we know that presidents can only serve two terms—a rule that was added to the Constitution for fear that the presidency would become a monarchy after Franklin Delano Roosevelt won a fourth term in office.[1] For Congress, monarchy is not the issue, but whether there should be a mandatory retirement for legislators is hotly debated.

Gerrymandering

In 2019, the US Supreme Court issued a much-awaited decision on political gerrymandering in a case called *Rucho v. Common Cause.*[2] Many people hoped the court would establish some red lines that politicians can't cross in drawing up congressional districts to entrench their own power. It didn't. Instead, the court said that it won't touch that hot potato—ever.

For starters, let's talk a bit about what gerrymandering is. Imagine a state with two districts. Imagine, too, that 75 percent of the voters in the state are registered Republicans who are spread out across the state. If the state were divided evenly down the middle to form two congressional districts, then two Republicans would probably go to the House of Representatives because the majority of voters across the entire state votes Republican.

Now imagine instead that voters living in the state's largest city are predominantly registered Democrats, while the rest of the state is predominantly Republican. The state legislature decides to carve up the state into one district made up of the city and its suburbs, effectively creating a Democratic stronghold, with the rest of the state constituting the second district. In that event, one Democrat and one Republican would go to the House, even though the majority of voters in the state are registered Republicans. This practice of creating politics-driven and oftentimes geographically illogical congressional districts is called *gerrymandering.*

In 1964, the Supreme Court ruled that House districts must be approximately equal *in population.*[3] Politicians can't carve up districts in a way that gives voters in sparsely populated districts more political power than those in densely populated districts. Otherwise, if you are voting for a member of the House of Representatives along with one million other people in District 1, for example, your vote would mean a lot less than your cousin who votes with only one hundred other people in District 2. After each census (which happens every ten years), districts are reconfigured to ensure that each person's vote counts roughly equally.

But imagine that two districts are carved up so that the populations of voters in District 1 and District 2 are basically equal, but the boundaries are drawn in such a tortured way as to artificially create a solid majority of Democrats in both. Republicans are sprinkled around in pockets so they will never have enough votes to elect a Republican member in any one district. Gerrymandering is not about the number of people in each district, but the number of people from a particular political party in each district. But if populations have to be fairly equal in number according to the Supreme Court, does the Constitution also require that they give voters from each party—in my example, Republicans—a fair shot at winning a district too?

The answer is: we will never know the answer. A 5–4 majority of the Supreme Court ruled in *Rucho* that drawing lines to help one *political party* and hurt another is not something federal courts can wade into.[4] The case involved two congressional districting plans—one in Maryland adopted by Democrats and one in North Carolina adopted by Republicans. In North Carolina, Representative David Lewis, a Republican cochair of the redistricting committee, sarcastically explained the redistricting criteria as follows: "We are drawing the maps to give partisan advantage to 10 Republicans and 3 Democrats because I do not believe it's possible to draw a map with 11 Republicans and 2 Democrats." When the plan was enacted on a party-line vote, the same Republican cochair announced: "I think electing Republicans is better than electing Democrats. So I drew this map to help foster what I think is better for the country." The plan worked.

Justice Elena Kagan dissented in *Rucho*, noting that "[t]he partisan gerrymandering in these cases deprived citizens of the most fundamental of their constitutional rights: the rights to participate equally in the political process, to join with others to advance political beliefs, and to choose their political representatives." She went on: "In so doing, the partisan gerrymanders here debased and dishonored our democracy, turning upside-down the core American idea that all governmental power derives from the people. These gerrymanders enabled politicians to entrench themselves in office as against voters' preferences. They promoted partisanship above respect for the popular will. They encouraged a politics of polarization and dysfunction. If left unchecked, gerrymanders like the ones here may irreparably damage our system of government."

The majority didn't disagree with Justice Kagan. It just decided that the federal courts can't play a part in figuring out what to do about it. As a consequence, if incumbent state politicians slice and dice congressional districts in ways that cement their own power—even if the voters want change—the Constitution can no longer be invoked in federal court to stop them. The majority in *Rucho* slammed the door on constitutional lawsuits seeking clarity on whether gerrymandered voting districts hurt voters under the Constitution. And the courthouse door is effectively shut forever—on the theory that the topic is too "political" for the courts, even if political gerrymandering amounts to a violation of the Constitution.

Gerrymandering questions are hard. The Constitution says nothing about Democrats or Republicans—or even political parties. If the Supreme Court were to devise a test for determining how to fairly divide districts among Democrats and Republicans, what would it look like? If there were more than two "major" political parties in America, would the Constitution require more congressional redistricting in order to divide the state "district pies" into *three* fair slices rather than just two? Fixing partisan gerrymandering only raises more questions.

The court's refusal to wade into that thicket—even if just to help fix the most egregious examples—is still troubling. The Supreme Court answers hard constitutional questions all the time. When it does, it formulates standards and tests even if they have no grounding in the text of the Constitution itself. Why is political gerrymandering any different? The court had taken up the constitutionality of congressional districts numerous times before—even deciding in 1993 that gerrymandering congressional districts based on *race* (versus political party) violates the Equal Protection Clause of the Constitution.[5] Why hold in 2019, then, that federal courts are essentially—and permanently—at a loss when it comes to deciding the limits of *partisan* gerrymandering under the Constitution? The answers the *Rucho* case gives to that question are not particularly satisfying.

You might be thinking: If gerrymandering is such an intractable cancer on American democracy and the federal courts can't be summoned to address it, why not just attack the problem at its source—that is, in the redistricting process itself? In the substantial majority of states with more than one district, the state legislatures decide how to carve up larger states into districts in the first place. State legislatures—like Congress—have members from both of the two major political parties. As in the US Congress, one of the two parties dominates either or both legislative chambers at the state level at any given point in time. If that party is the Republican Party, legislatures will likely divide up the congressional districts in a way that maximizes the possibility that Republicans will go to the House. And vice versa—if state legislatures are controlled by the Democratic Party at time of a reapportionment, they will likely carve up districts in ways that maximize representation in Congress by Democrats. (It can also matter who is in the governor's office with veto power, but hopefully you get the point.) So in essence, the Supreme Court's decision in *Rucho* sent the partisan gerrymandering problem back to partisan gerrymandered politicians—fallaciously expecting them to simply do the right thing.

Here's the good news. As of May 2019, eight states—Alaska, Arizona, California, Colorado, Idaho, Michigan, Montana, and Washington—have formed independent, nonpartisan commissions whose job it is to develop maps of the legislative districts following the census every ten years, instead of state legislatures. Independent commissions vary in terms of the number of commissioners, how they are chosen, and what kind of vote is needed to approve a redistricting map. In 2015, the US Supreme Court held that the use of independent commissions for redistricting purposes is constitutional, rejecting the state of Arizona's argument that the Constitution should be read literally when it authorizes "the Legislature" to decide how to hold elections for the House of Representative and the Senate.[6]

If partisan gerrymandering is to be fixed, then, voters have to demand independent redistricting processes. As mentioned before, at the end of the day, if American government is going to change, voters have to demand it—at the ballot box. There's really no other way.

Term Limits for Congress

Now for a few words about term limits for members of Congress—or the lack thereof. Unlike for the president, who can only serve two terms in office under the Twenty-Second Amendment to the Constitution, there are no term limits for members of Congress in the Constitution. Senators can serve what amounts to a lifetime of six-year terms, and House members can serve a lifetime of two-year terms. The late Democratic senator Robert C. Byrd served West Virginia in Congress for over fifty-one years, and John Dingell Jr.—another Democrat—served sixty years in the House. Nearly every Congress since 1943 has attempted to impose term limits on itself, and nearly three-quarters of likely voters favor such a measure, but none has succeeded.

Why are term limits such a big issue? It's no secret that members of Congress increasingly spend their time "dialing for dollars" rather than actually proposing and enacting legislation that would benefit the voting public. If they knew their time in office was limited, members would be more willing to take political risks for the sake of their voters. If politicians aren't constantly worried about raising money and making donors happy, they will focus on what really should matter: voters. New faces in Congress also mean new ideas, while incumbent politicians may be habitually reelected even if they are no longer the best qualified for office. Overall, the argument goes, term limits on Congress could make Congress more effective at lawmaking and more legitimate in the eyes of the American public. If members are focused more on individual voters' needs and desires and less on deep-pocket donors, every American's vote—and the right to vote itself—is enhanced. So long as members of Congress are focused on dollar signs to extend their own careers in office, we will not achieve democracy by "We the People."

The arguments on the other side are also formidable. Those who oppose term limits point out that voters reelect their members every two or six years, depending on whether a race is in the House or in the Senate. To deny them their preferred candidate—even if that person has been in office for numerous terms—is to marginalize their vote, not enhance it. Moreover, legislating and navigating the halls of Congress is a skill that requires experience and expertise. Arbitrarily forcing people out of office to be replaced by newbies with no knowledge of how Congress works could backfire. Finally, some argue that term limits would make members of Congress more—not less—susceptible to wealthy and powerful donors. With more experienced members out the door, the best source of expertise for new members of Congress will be long-standing lobbyists, many of whom are former members themselves.[7]

Because the American experiment has never included term limits for Congress, it's impossible to predict whether they would help or harm the integrity of American democracy. It's hard to dispute, however, that the current system isn't working well for regular voters.

DISCUSSION QUESTIONS FOR CHAPTER 8

- If you had to defend partisan gerrymandering, how might you do it? Are there favorable reasons for allowing politicians to cement power in one party? After all, nothing in the Constitution bans the practice.

- Gerrymandering raises bigger questions about whether the two-party system of government itself is a problem for democracy by "We the People." What arguments might you make in favor of a multiparty system? Given that gerrymandering cannot be resolved through the courts, what other ways might voters fix the problems with party-led politics?

- Can you think of an analogy in everyday life that helps you understand better the pros and cons of term limits for Congress? Some religious denominations, law firms, and corporations have a mandatory retirement age for leadership, for example. Do those analogies help clarify your point of view regarding whether term limits for Congress would be good or bad for American democracy?

9

Does Your Vote Even Matter? Senate Malapportionment and Winner-Takes-All Vote Counting

Chapter 9 Takeaway Box

- Each state only gets two senators. This means that voters in bigger states matter less in the Senate than voters in smaller states. It's unfair, but it's in the Constitution.

- The winner-takes-all rule of vote-counting means that lots of votes may be wasted. This happens in presidential races and in elections to the House of Representatives.
- These problems must be fixed, if at all, by voting.

The last chapter mentioned that the Supreme Court considers *population*-based gerrymandering unconstitutional. The rationale is that drawing districts so that some votes have more value than others is at odds with the Equal Protection Clause of the US Constitution. Some call this the "one person, one vote" rule—the idea is that Jessica's vote doesn't get to "count" more than Jerome's just because Jerome lives in a more populated district. But the glaring contradiction with the one person, one vote rule is this: by definition, the Constitution's two-senator-per-state rule allows some people's votes to count a lot more than the votes of other people, depending on who lives in highly populated or less-populated states.

In addition to discussing Senate malapportionment, this chapter addresses the wonky problem of how to actually "count" votes once they are cast. By "count," I don't mean the literal tallying of the number of people who voted for a particular candidate. That part is straightforward, but sometimes bungled. The question is how to weigh the total votes cast for a candidate in a particular district or state for purposes of a broader election. Does that candidate get a *percentage* of the total vote—with smaller percentages going to less popular candidates? Or does the candidate essentially get handed the *entire* state for purposes of the broader election on the theory that majority rule wins?

Again, these issues bear on the broader question that this book asks but cannot possibly answer: What does the "right" to vote actually mean when it comes to choosing elected officials? Does your own vote "count" as much as it should? And if not, how to make it "count" more?

Senate Malapportionment

Senate malapportionment is a big and clumsy term, but it basically comes down to fairness. Enormously populated states like California (thirty-nine million) get the same representation in the Senate as low-population states like Wyoming (579,000). This is significant, in part because it means that individuals who live in highly populated states have a relatively weaker voice in the Senate than people who live in sparsely populated states. Because states are awarded electoral votes based on the number of representatives in the House of Representatives and the Senate, voters in smaller, less-populated states get more of a say in the Electoral College—and in deciding the presidency—than those in larger-populated states.[1]

This wasn't a given. At the constitutional convention in the summer of 1787, delegates from large states endorsed James Madison's Virginia Plan, which would have based Senate representation on state populations. The bigger the population, the more senators a state would get. The argument was that larger states contributed more to the government's financial coffers than smaller states, so their voters should have a relatively larger say in what goes on in the Senate. Instead, the delegates to the convention narrowly agreed to give states equal votes in the Senate to protect the relative power of each state on a national scale. They also debated how many senators to allow per state, ultimately settling on two.[2]

The Senate wields an extraordinary amount of power relative to the House of Representatives. The nation saw this phenomenon when Senate Majority Leader Mitch McConnell refused to bring President Barack Obama's US Supreme Court nominee to the Senate floor and, more recently, when it acquitted President Trump of impeachment charges. The president's power to appoint public officials—including members of her cabinet, ambassadors, and federal judges—is contingent on the Senate's advice and consent. The Constitution also requires the advice and consent of the Senate for the president to make treaties (although as a practical matter, presidents can make things that look like treaties without Senate involvement). The Constitution doesn't define what "advice and consent" means, but as a practical matter, the Senate holds hearings to question the appointee prior to a vote—first in the Senate Judiciary Committee and then in the full Senate.

Starting with a Democratic-controlled Senate in 2013, nominees for the vitally important job of serving as a federal (versus state) judge have cleared the Senate by a simple majority vote, regardless of opposition by the minority party. Although the current confirmation process is not required by the Constitution, internal Senate procedures effectively allowed McConnell to stop President Obama—and the American voter constituency he represented—from exercising his constitutional power to appoint a Supreme Court justice. Similarly, the 50 percent majority rule for confirmation of federal judges means that the minority party in the Senate—and its voters—don't really matter when it comes to confirming Supreme Court justices to office.

The Senate is also a gatekeeper to legislation getting to the president's desk. Even if the more representative body (i.e., the House) might want something passed, it can be killed in the Senate. And recall that a citizen of Wyoming, the least populous state in the country, has a Senate voting power sixty-seven times that of a citizen of the largest state: California.[3] And because the Senate majority leader decides whether to bring legislation to the floor of the Senate for consideration in the first place, voters in that person's state—Kentucky, as of this book's writing—effectively have much more power over American government than voters in any other state in America. Because if the Senate majority leader refuses to bring a bill to the Senate floor—even a bipartisan one—that bill is dead, even if a majority of the American public favors it.

The Senate is also the body that acts as the jury that decides at an impeachment trial whether a president should be acquitted or convicted and removed from office. The House merely establishes the charges against the president (or other officers who are subject to impeachment under the Constitution). The charges are called "articles of impeachment." Like the Constitution itself, this piece of paper is meaningless without enforcement, which can only occur in the Senate. The House of Representatives issued articles of impeachment against President Bill Clinton, for example, and the Senate refused to convict. By contrast, President Richard Nixon resigned from office when he realized that, if his impeachment went to trial in the Senate, he would lose.[4] Some argue that the failed impeachment trial conviction of Bill Clinton gutted the Impeachment Clause of its force and effect, morphing it into a political stunt destined to fall flat with future voters and future presidents.[5] With President Trump's impeachment by the House of Representatives and acquittal in the Senate, impeachment as a meaningful check on presidential abuses may well be dead.

Imagine, though, if the number of state senators—like the number of members of the House of Representatives—were weighted according to population. Things would be very different in American government. The two-senator rule means that the US population could have a Republican-led Senate for a long time, even if a majority of American voters want change.[6] The problem with this scenario is that attitudes and policies change over time. Healthy debate and varied viewpoints often produce better outcomes. Think of your own everyday life. If your mom needs to decide whether to undergo a life-threatening surgery, you might insist that she consult trusted friends and family members, as well as multiple medical professionals, to be sure that she makes the right decision. You might even make a "pros and cons" list with her. A gut call on whether to undergo surgery—based on preconceived biases and ideology—would be dangerous. At the top echelons of government, too, better decision-making happens with informed debate. If nobody is around to lay the cons on the table, some bad—and long-lasting—decisions can happen.

All told, because of the extraordinary power that senators wield and their disproportionate representation of individual voters, some people have called for an amendment to the Constitution to change the two-senator-per-state rule, on the rationale that it unfairly entrenches too much power in incumbent senators who are difficult to unseat. Others have argued that huge states like California should be divided into smaller states, each with their own two senators in Congress, so that voters in more populated states have fairer representation in the Senate.[7] Under Article V of the Constitution, changing the configuration of the Senate would require a constitutional amendment, which would itself require a two-thirds vote in both houses of Congress and ratification by three-quarters of the states' legislatures. That's exceedingly tough to do, particularly in the "no compromise" culture of modern politics.

Winner-Takes-All Vote Counting

Even if a person manages to register, to show up at the proper polling place with the proper ID, and to vote, the impact of that vote could be washed out. (But once again, before you become disheartened, remember that if you don't vote, you are effectively throwing in the towel on the privilege of American democracy, which deserves our full-throated support!)

Most voting systems at the local state and federal levels—including the District of Columbia and forty-eight states for purposes of the Electoral College—are "winner-takes-all" systems. The winning candidate must get either a majority of the votes (50 percent) or what's called a plurality—in a three-way race, for example, the winner would have to get the highest percentage of votes, even if that is less than 50 percent (for example, candidate A would get 42 percent versus candidate B's 35 percent and candidate C's 23 percent). What this means is that a slim majority decides everything—rendering the minority votes a waste. They get wiped out.

In presidential elections, this is one reason why swing states are the only ones that get any attention—in heavy "red" or "blue" states, candidates know that changing a few votes won't change the majority tally. Because all electors go with the majority, why bother courting minority voters in the first place? The winner-takes-all rule also means that minority party voters in elections to the House of Representatives don't matter a whole lot, either. If 50.1 percent of voters in a congressional district choose candidate A, then 100 percent of that district will be represented by candidate A. Because so few voters participate in US elections—particularly in years when the presidential contest is not in play—it means that the House of Representatives is chosen only by the majority of the minority of voters who participated in the first place.[8]

The major alternative to winner-takes-all systems is one widely used in western Europe. Instead of having a single winner in each district, a "proportional representation" (PR) voting system clumps a bunch of districts and candidates together, and the *party* that gets the most votes across all districts is allotted more seats in the legislature than the losing party. In Nebraska and Maine, proportional voting applies. So it's possible that candidate A would win one district (and thus one electoral vote) and candidate B would win another district (and thus one electoral vote). Rather than sending all electors to the Electoral College on behalf of one candidate who won the statewide majority, electors cast votes for different presidential candidates in proportion to what the voters want.[9]

California has fifty-three congressional districts for the House of Representatives. Each of those districts picks one candidate, usually either a Republican or Democrat. But imagine that Californians instead all voted together, casting individual votes either for the Republican Party or the Democratic Party. Imagine, too, that 60 percent of the voters choose the Republicans' platform, and 40 percent choose the Democrats' platform. In that event, thirty-two Republicans would go to Congress and twenty-one Democrats would go to Congress.

In short, a PR system ranks voters' choices, and people are sent to the legislature based on that ranking—not based on an up-or-down vote for each candidate. According to the nonpartisan organization FairVote, the benefits of a PR system over a winner-takes-all system include "more accurate representation of parties, better representation for political and racial minorities, fewer wasted votes, higher levels of voter turnout, better representation of women, greater likelihood of majority rule, and little opportunity for gerrymandering."[10] Matthew Yglesias of Vox likewise explains that, under a PR system, "you wouldn't get anything like the current situation anymore, where 30 percent of the voters in Massachusetts backed Trump and 30 percent of the voters in Oklahoma backed Clinton, but Massachusetts returns a uniformly Democratic house delegation and Oklahoma returns a uniformly Republican one. Relatedly, but not identically, you'd basically eliminate gerrymandering as a factor in American public affairs."[11]

There have been a number of efforts to change the winner-takes-all system, which is a politically controversial subject. After all, at the presidential level, the winner-takes-all rule has helped four Republicans get elected notwithstanding a contrary popular vote—Rutherford B. Hayes in 1876, Benjamin Harrison in 1888, George W. Bush in 2000, and Donald Trump in 2016.[12] So far, sixteen states have signed onto the National Popular Vote Interstate Compact, agreeing to have all their respective electors cast Electoral College votes according to the national popular vote. The compact kicks in if enough states join such that, taken together, they cross the 270 threshold needed to elect a president.[13] And in 2018, a series of lawsuits were filed in federal courts to strike down winner-takes-all laws as unconstitutional and in violation of the one person, one vote rule—which is a difficult legal argument to win.[14]

Of course, the other way to change the system is to change the underlying state laws mandating a winner-takes-all process. That requires voting for politicians who support an alternative. Once again, friends: it all comes down to the precious right—or prerogative—to vote.

DISCUSSION QUESTIONS FOR CHAPTER 9

- After reading the last two chapters, how are you feeling about your right to vote? If you are feeling defeated, why? If you are feeling emboldened, why? If there was one thing you could change about the system so far, what would it be?

- Do you think that the original reason for having two senators per state—that is, to make sure that the smaller states aren't drowned out by the larger states in Congress—makes sense today? If the Senate configuration can't be changed except by a constitutional amendment, what alterations might you make to the Senate's internal rules for deciding how it does its business?

- In the 2012 documentary *Electoral Dysfunction*, political humorist Mo Rocca did a mock election with elementary school kids, tasking them with deciding which was best—colored pencils or markers.[15] The popular vote went to markers, but the Electoral College vote went to colored pencils, so colored pencils won the election. The losing kids were incensed. Does their outrage make sense to you on a human level? If so, do you think the winner-takes-all system should go? What should take its place?

10

Money in Politics

Chapter 10 Takeaway Box

- Federal campaign finance laws are designed to make sure politicians answer to voters—not big money donors.
- In general, **campaigns** can spend all they want because the First Amendment allows them to.
- In general, **people** and **organizations** cannot donate all they want to campaigns, because

Congress doesn't want politicians answering to big donors once they're in office. They should be working for the people.

- At least four workarounds to this last rule have emerged, however. They include soft money, PACs, super PACs, and hard money. These forces flood federal campaigns with money anyway—and it's not coming from individual voters.

We hear a lot in the news about "campaign finance reform." Many of us tune it out as wonky and boring. But what does that term really mean? And why should regular people care?

Think again about how American government—that is, government by "We the People"—is supposed to work. The idea is that there is no single government boss with divine power from high above. The bosses are dispersed among a bunch of officeholders, and their power comes from the people. We voters get to decide who is in government and we get to shape what actions those people do and don't take while they're in government. We do this by voting. Politicians comply with the wishes of the voters because they want to keep their jobs. That's the theory, anyway.

We all know how this works from our common everyday experience. You show up to work on time every day—barring some unexpected crisis—because you want to keep your job. Students show up to class on time because they want to pass the class. In the real world, there are consequences for not doing what we are "supposed" to do. We conform our behavior to avoid those consequences.

Now think about politicians. The question that campaign finance reform raises is: Who is *really* their boss, and what are the consequences if they don't do what they're supposed to do? Are they actually making decisions in office based on what voters want—for fear of getting fired in the next election? Or are they making decisions based on some other, behind-the-scenes boss? Many people believe the answer to the last question is yes, and that the real boss is money. Politicians want more money in order to win campaigns and stay in office; when winning is about a money chase, what voters want becomes secondary.

The purpose of campaign finance laws at their core is to make sure that politicians don't take or spend money improperly and that voters are able to keep track of the money they do take and spend. If the proverbial "bad guy"—think of a mob boss or a corrupt foreign government that wants to control American politics—is able to pay off politicians with campaign dollars behind a veil of secrecy, then democracy won't work anymore. "We the People"—and our needs and desires—lose our voice in government, because money is really doing the talking.

Here's what you need to know about what federal laws are in place to stave off this distortion of democracy: it comes down to the difference between money *paid into* a campaign, and money *paid out of* a campaign. The US Supreme Court has said that Congress can limit money paid *into* a campaign. But the court has said that Congress can't regulate or limit how politicians and their campaigns (and outside groups not connected to candidates) *spend* money out of a campaign to get their messages out.[1] Let's break this down a bit further, into three basic principles.

The first is what I'll call the **sky's-the-limit payout principle**. The law allows candidates for office to spend whatever they want. That's because spending money to get yourself elected is considered free speech protected under the First Amendment. There's one hitch: the law requires that candidates disclose a bunch of information to the federal agency charged with overseeing campaigns and elections—the Federal Election Commission (FEC)—including lists of donors and the amounts the donors contribute to candidates.[2] The idea here is that voters should know who is actually funding a candidate's campaign, so that they can take that information into account at the voting booth. If you don't like who is lining a politician's pockets, you might vote for someone else. But if you don't know who the source of money is in the first place, you can't cast your vote accordingly.

The second is what I'll call the **limited pay-in principle**. Individual people can only pay a limited amount of money into a campaign. Corporations, unions, and foreigners can't contribute into a campaign at all. Congress is the source of these laws. The problem that these laws try to fix is the classic quid pro quo.[3] Without the laws, a candidate might quietly agree as follows: "Dear donor, if you give me money so I can win this election, then once I'm in office, I'll use my power to do favors for you or your political causes, regardless of what's best for the voters."

The third is what I'll call the **workarounds**. Candidates will always want money, and donors will always want influence. That much is for certain. So they've figured out ways to get around the limited pay-in principle. Instead of donating a bunch of money to the campaign, why not just run your own ads totally separate from the campaign? That's free speech too, right? In other words, instead of you giving candidate Jamal money to run an ad saying, "Vote for Jamal," just run the ad all by yourself saying, "Vote for Jamal." Imagine that Congress bans this kind of express advocacy on behalf of a candidate (which it did).[4] Instead of running an ad saying "Vote for Jamal," you run an ad saying "Jamal's opponent is horrible," or

"Jamal will fix your health care." (These kinds of ads are called issue ads.)

Either way, so long as Jamal-the-candidate has nothing to do with your decision to run an ad favoring his candidacy, and so long as you run an ad that's about issues and not an ad that contains express advocacy for or against electing Jamal, there's no quid pro quo problem, right? He can't do you favors in exchange for something he wasn't party to.

Before you answer this, let's switch up the hypothetical a bit. What if, instead of being an actual human being, the "you" in this scenario is a corporation? Let's say, too, that the corporation wants to drill for oil in an environmentally protected Arctic region of America. Jamal is down for drilling. So the corporation runs ads for Jamal—leaving Jamal totally out of the loop. Is that scenario any different—any more or less problematic—than if an individual is running the ads? After all, Jamal knows where the support is coming from.

One difference might be that individuals have First Amendment rights because we are living, breathing human beings who can physically be thrown in jail or even executed by the government if our rights are violated. Rights in the Constitution are about confining government power so that the government can't trample on regular people arbitrarily. Corporations are legal fictions, which are essentially designed to preserve assets. They are not people or even buildings. They are not tangible things. They are legal abstractions.

We might say, too, that corporations running ads for Jamal are more troubling than a human being running an ad for Jamal. Corporations don't vote. They aren't part of "We the People" who form and control our own government. Again, they are legal fictions whose purpose is to make money. Individuals have families and jobs and bodies that need to stay healthy. Individual human beings care about things more than just making money—because they have to. So when individuals run ads for Jamal, it makes sense as a matter of democracy to let them do that, in addition to protecting individual rights under the First Amendment.

Well, the Supreme Court, in a famous decision called *Citizens United v. FEC* in 2010, disagreed with the above distinction and reiterated that corporations do have First Amendment rights. This means that they can run issue ads all they want—so long as they don't coordinate with a candidate.[5] The law still bans corporations from contributing to or coordinating directly with the candidate herself, so the quid pro quo problem is not a problem, right? Well, many people would say, "wrong." Many people would say that corporations and candidates know exactly how they can scratch each other's backs even if they can't talk about it directly. Many would say that when a corporation runs an ad for Jamal that touts drilling in the Arctic, Jamal knows full well that when he gets elected he will have to tend to the demands of the corporation that helped get him there. He will have to vote for Arctic drilling—even if a majority of the actual human beings in his voting constituency oppose it. Another way of saying this (which I use a lot in my law school classrooms) is that it's a little too "cute" to suggest that there is no quid pro quo going on here. We all have common sense.

Bottom line: so long as a campaign issue ad isn't coordinated with a candidate, it's fair game and unlimited under federal law. All this leeway has led to a surge of spending on campaigns and elections from entities other than actual campaigns—what's known as "outside spending." This is the big problem with our campaign finance system. Outside spending has skyrocketed, and there is no accountability whatsoever for it.

As a result, a person who wants to run for office only has to think about two things when it comes to campaign finance: managing *direct* contributions (which today are capped at $2,700 per person to an individual candidate), and making disclosures to the FEC.[6] Even these limits have their critics. Some people don't even want laws that mandate transparency in campaigns. It's hard to understand how transparency harms individual voters. As the saying goes, sunshine is the best disinfectant. But in thinking about federal campaign finance laws, it's important to keep in mind that there are politicians in office who want no legal restrictions whatsoever on money in federal campaigns. Why? Because they are worried that regulating campaign spending—speech that is at the heart of our political dialogue—risks burdening free speech. Cynics point out that this pro–free speech, laissez-faire approach to campaign finance law tends to favor large corporations over regular people, and that politicians who disfavor campaign finance laws are really committed to maximizing the flow of corporate money for their next campaign.

Now let's clear up some more terminology:

When donations are made directly to a campaign or a candidate, they're called **hard money**. (This is the money captured by what I earlier called the "limited pay-in principle.") Under federal law, you can give money to candidates, political parties, and other entities, but only so much. Foreigners, corporations, and unions can't make any hard-money donations.

To get around hard-money limits, the "workarounds" emerged. There are four of them. The first is called **soft money**, which is money given to political *parties* instead of candidates. Soft money comes from individuals, but not directly from corporations or their treasury funds, on the theory that it's about party-building, not helping individual candidates. But a law passed in 2002 called the Bipartisan Campaign Reform Act—also known as "BCRA," or "McCain-Feingold," after the bill's sponsors, Arizona senator John McCain and Wisconsin senator Russ Feingold—effectively banned individual soft money contributions. After McCain-Feingold, political parties had to fund ads with hard money. Ads also must include a disclaimer that the candidate "approves the message."[7]

Corporations are not out of the donation loop as a result of the hard money ban, however. They are allowed to siphon off small amounts of money from shareholders and give it directly to campaigns through what are called **political action committees**, or **PACs**—the second in our list of workaround principles. PACs are separate, segregated funds that are created mostly by corporations and unions. They must register with the FEC. Remember that corporations and unions can't directly contribute hard money to actual campaigns. So PACs collect funds from union members or from corporate shareholders, aggregate those funds, and then give directly to campaigns instead. PACs can't take money from groups, and individuals can only give up to $5,000 to a PAC. Moreover, PACs can only give up to $5,000 in hard money per candidate in primary and general elections.[8] Independent PACs can solicit money from the general public too. There are thousands of PACs today. The US Chamber of Commerce has a PAC, for example, as does Microsoft, the Teamsters, and the National Rifle Association (NRA).[9]

There are two more workarounds to be aware of. Recall that PACs can only give a certain amount of money to campaigns and they can only accept a certain amount of money from donors. After a 5–4 majority of the Supreme Court held in *Citizens United* that corporations can spend an unlimited amount of money on campaign ads, a third workaround known as the **super PAC** came about.[10] Super PACs can raise and spend unlimited amounts of money. And they can accept money from organizations—unlike PACs. Super PACs are still regulated by the FEC, so they must disclose their donors and how they're spending money. But unlike PACs, super PACs can't *ever* give money to campaigns.

Like PACs, super PACs cannot coordinate with campaigns, either. But they've found a way to bypass the statutory contribution limits to campaigns. Instead of giving $5,000 to a campaign through a PAC, a corporation can give, say, $50 million in unrestricted spending on the airwaves through a super PAC. So long as the super PAC does not discuss its plans with the candidate it favors or coordinate in any way, that super PAC can spend whatever it wants to get its candidate elected. In short, super PACs are independent entities that can spend as much money as they want to run ads on TV and other media outlets. Moreover, a super PAC can collect as much money as it wants from persons or groups—including corporations and unions.[11] Because super PAC donors can be groups, the actual people behind super PACs can be hard to identify, leaving voters—and even candidates—in the dark as to who is funding a candidate. But one thing is for sure: when ad money starts flooding into competitive districts from nowhere, it means a super PAC has gotten involved in a campaign.

The fourth workaround is known as **dark money**. This term sounds ominous, as it should. Dark money is a form of outside money that flows through what's called a section 501(c)(4) entity, which is a reference to the US tax code's provisions allowing for the creation of nonprofit organizations and social welfare groups. These entities can raise and spend an unlimited amount of money. And unlike a super PAC, a 501(c)(4) doesn't have to disclose where it gets the money—only what it spends. Because they are technically nonprofit entities, section 501(c)(4) organizations can only spend 49.9 percent of their time on politics. The rest of their time must be spent on other things—like holding annual meetings. The NRA and Planned Parenthood are both section 501(c)(4) organizations. And they both spend a lot of time and money on campaigns and elections.

To recap, then: PACs have to disclose donors, but donors *can't* be organizations like corporations or unions. Super PACs have to disclose donors, but donors *can* be organizations, so it's hard to tell who is exactly behind the money spent on super PAC ads. It doesn't help that they can have innocuous-sounding names like "We Love America." (Comedian Stephen Colbert even created a real super PAC he called Americans for a Better Tomorrow, Tomorrow.) Section 501(c)(4) organizations don't have to disclose their donors at all because they aren't even campaign-related entities—they are entities created under the tax code.

If you want to spend an unlimited amount of money on a campaign, then call yourself a nonprofit group or social welfare organization, hire a lawyer to make sure you are filing the right forms with the IRS, and then be sure that more than half of your work isn't campaign-related. Presto! You've worked around what remains of the federal campaign laws. This is what dark money is about. Although section 501(c)(4) groups have long been exempt from disclosing funding sources, it wasn't until *Citizens United* that people who wanted to spend large sums of money on political campaigns without having to disclose who they were started to create "nonprofit" groups to engage in electoral politics anonymously.

Another form of tax-exempt organization that can operate to influence elections is known as a "527 group"—named after section 527 of the Internal Revenue Code that governs them. A 527 group can engage in electoral politics without the percentage restrictions of 501(c)(4) organizations. There are no limits on the source and amount of legal contributions to 527s, either. But 527 organizations must register with the IRS and publicly disclose their donors and spending, and they cannot expressly advocate for any particular candidates or coordinate with campaigns. Many PACs and super PACs are in fact nonprofit organizations created under section 527 of the US tax code.[12]

Now, you might be saying, what about the FEC? Isn't it supposed to be watching over all this stuff? The answer is yes and no. The no stems in part from the fact that the FEC arguably has no power to oversee organizations created as tax-exempt organizations under the Internal Revenue Code, as long as they don't expressly advocate for or against a candidate or coordinate with a campaign. It's the IRS's job to keep track of nonprofit organizations, but it can only audit nonprofits to ensure they are not engaging in prohibited political activity. The IRS does not have the power to regulate campaigns more generally. If the tax-exempt loophole is to be fixed, Congress must do it—and Congress is so polarized these days that it isn't in the business of making or fixing many substantive laws regarding politically charged issues.

Plus, as I mentioned earlier, some people in Congress are very opposed to having any restrictions on the financing of federal campaigns—they think campaign finance laws are an affront to the First Amendment. Of course, the First Amendment does not forbid all limits on speech. People can't jokingly yell "fire" in a crowded theater and avoid problems with the police on the rationale that they have a First Amendment right to free speech. Constitutional rights are routinely limited by other important public policy objectives, including public safety. Exercising free speech through campaign dollars is no different. The question is how to balance the free speech objective with other important, competing objectives—such as ensuring that campaigns are fair and that, for regular people, the right to vote is meaningful. (Keep in mind, too, that states have their own campaign finance laws, which vary tremendously and are thus a topic for another day.)[13]

The other problem with the FEC has to do with the structure of the agency itself. Imagine that a campaign fails to disclose its donors, in violation of a US statute. Normally, we'd need a cop on the block to issue a citation and prosecute a violation of the law. For campaign finance laws, that cop is the FEC. But the FEC is headed by a panel, not a person. It has three commissioners from the Democratic Party and three commissioners from the Republican Party. Congress set it up this way and mandated the 3–3 composition. The result? Partisan deadlocks. Presidents can further defang the FEC by refusing to appoint new commissioners when people leave. The FEC cannot function without a quorum of four people. Currently, the number of commissioners has dropped to three.[14] Even if those three wanted to take an action against a campaign or entity that was blatantly violating the law, they can't. There aren't enough people on the job, and there's nothing in the law requiring the president to fill vacancies. It's in a president's personal interests to keep that cop off the block while he is in office.

All told, consider this contradiction: as an individual, you can only give $2,700 to a campaign (as of the date of this writing). The rationale behind the limit is that, if you could give more, you could unduly influence a politician once he's in office. By comparison, Amazon or Shell Oil (and individual millionaires or billionaires) can spend an unlimited amount of money to flood the airwaves and the internet with ads favoring or criticizing a candidate. Candidates know this and they might even know where that money is coming from. There's a ban on your donation dollars, but not on corporate America's. You could run your own ads, of course, and many very rich people do. But let's face it—for most of us, the corporate coffers have ours beat. You tell me: Which is the greater threat to democracy—your 2,701st-dollar donation to candidate Jamal? Or the billions spent by unidentified deep pockets on "independent" advertising aimed at getting your neighbor to vote for or against Jamal?

DISCUSSION QUESTIONS FOR CHAPTER 10

- What is the most important thing you learned from this chapter? Is it that campaigns can spend whatever they want? Or that individuals can only contribute $2,700 to a campaign? Or that dark money—basically, unidentified bank accounts with gobs of money—can spend an unlimited amount on air convincing you to vote for or against a candidate?

- Do you think campaign finance limitations are a good idea in general? We didn't get into the statutory background or the rationale much in this chapter, but bear in mind that the law requires a certain amount of transparency so that we know how campaigns are getting and spending money. But with the workarounds, those laws aren't really doing much to keep campaigns influence-free—the airwaves are dominated by big cash anyway. Do you agree or disagree with this last proposition? Why?

- If you believe that some measure of government oversight over the financing of federal campaigns is worthwhile, how might we go about amending the federal campaign laws to make things more fair for individual voters? Or has *Citizens United* made it too hard for Congress to do anything, now that corporations can invoke the First Amendment to protect their ability to spend, spend, spend? Some people believe that the only option to the problem of money in politics is a constitutional amendment overruling *Citizens United* and confining corporate spending on campaigns. But constitutional amendments are nearly impossible to achieve.

11

Voter Suppression and Voter Fraud: Myths or Realities?

Chapter 11 Takeaway Box

- Data-driven studies show that voter fraud is a myth.
- New state laws make it harder and harder for eligible voters to vote—on the false rationale that voter fraud is a problem in America.

- Be wary of politicians' motives, even those from your political party of choice. As the framers of the Constitution understood, it's human nature to amass and retain individual power—even at the price of democracy by "We the People."

Before reading this book, you—like me—might have assumed that the right to vote is pretty much a "given" in America, and that pretty much everyone agrees that it's a given. The reality is not so. Politicians have long waged—and continue to wage—a stealth battle in America over whether people should be allowed to vote or whether they should be kept from voting. This battle is not about fairness or democracy or what's best for individuals and their families. It's mostly about keeping power in the ranks of the already powerful.

This chapter covers two things: what's known as "voter suppression," and its counterpoint, which is called "voter fraud." These are controversial topics. And implicitly, they tend to be treated as two sides of the same coin.

Some people argue that imposing legal requirements on registration and voting operate to suppress the vote—either by making it logistically harder for people to vote or by killing people's incentive to vote and fostering cynicism about the entire process. It's a way of shoring up power for the already powerful.

On the other side of the coin is the argument that having to comply with certain legal requirements to cast a vote is part and parcel of living in modern society. We have to deal with red tape all the time. Widening the door to the ballot box would wreak all kinds of havoc on the results of an election—the wrong people would be deciding our democracy when it should be "We the People."

For the second group of people, only the "right" people should have the right to vote. This group isn't necessarily trying to exclude people from voting. They may be seriously concerned that people who should not be voting will vote if the rules are too relaxed.

Let's tease this out a bit.

Recall that under the Constitution, states basically get to make the rules for how their own residents vote. Some states are liberal with their voting requirements. Some are stricter. We need official identification to do lots of things in modern American society, like getting on a plane or opening a bank account. What's the big deal, then, with requiring people to have proper identification in order to register to vote, and then to actually vote? If you can't get your act together to show a poll worker that you are who you say you are, then you shouldn't be casting a vote in something as important as an election. It's government by "We the People," after all. Fakers need not apply.

This argument makes a lot of sense on its own, but unfortunately the issue is more nuanced and complicated. Recall, too, that this country was founded on the premise inherent in human nature: that people in power will strive to protect that power and to amass more of it. That's why we have a three-part system of separated powers at the federal level and an entirely separate system of state sovereigns. Ratified in 1788, the original Constitution only allowed one category of people to vote: white males who were wealthy enough to own land. This group held all the political power. If we accept the commonsense notion that those in power want to hang on to it, it's not hard to accept the commonsense notion that expanding the pool of voters is tricky business. The more voters, the more diluted the power of the existing voting class—and existing politicians—becomes. People in power feel threatened if a swarm of new faces have a say in whether they should stay in power.

So it's perhaps no big surprise that it took many, many years for the pool of eligible voters to expand from white male landowners to white males who didn't own land, then to formerly enslaved men of color, and then, in the early twentieth century, to women. These were hard-fought battles, and it's folly to assume that, once the words of the Constitution were amended to open the voting tent to more categories of humans, the war over voting was totally over. History instead shows that—particularly for African Americans—the traditional power holders sought to keep new voters from the polls anyway. Those in power got "cute" and made up excuses to keep people from the polls even though they knew the law required them to afford access. The Constitution, after all, is just a piece of paper. It won't enforce itself. So if the "cuteness" principle means anything, it means that people will try to get around even the Constitution's limitations—and will get away with it if there are no consequences for doing so.

During the Jim Crow era, in which state and local laws were enacted to enforce racial segregation in the American South, poll taxes and literacy tests operated to outmaneuver the right to vote. The constitutional right to vote didn't mean much under these regimes because the barriers to entry were too high. This is just common sense. Imagine, by comparison, that a sports recruiter tells a 110-pound woman that she can apply for the position of a linebacker for a professional football team. It looks like a fair offer on paper, but of course, a small woman doesn't have the physical strength to satisfy the qualifications for that job, so the job "opportunity" itself is bunk.

Same too with voting. If a low-income person has $600 per month to feed and house a family of four, and it costs $100 to register to vote (taking into consideration the costs of getting the requisite paperwork, such as a certified copy of a birth certificate and so on), then the "right" to vote is practically meaningless. Same goes for literacy tests. If a person could not read because she lacked access to education, or if she could read but the questions were so esoteric as to be unanswerable (such as "How many bubbles are in a bar of soap?"—a real question on a southern state's literacy test in the twentieth century), then the constitutional right to vote amounts to nothing.[1]

By the mid-twentieth century, Congress realized that this was the state of affairs—notwithstanding passage of various constitutional amendments broadening the voting tent to allow more people access to the polls. So it passed the Voting Rights Act in 1965. That statute addressed many barriers to voting that states had erected to keep newcomers from the polls. The law worked as intended—and for many years, the states had a harder time successfully passing restrictions on individuals' ready-access to the voting booth.

But in 2013, the Supreme Court by a 5–4 vote struck down a critical piece of that legislation, opening the door to new laws that effectively operate to make it harder for people to vote.[2] The court signaled that Congress was free to try again with a new statute, but our polarized federal legislature hasn't achieved that, which—unfortunately—is hardly surprising these days. (In December 2019, a bill did pass the House of Representatives that would restore parts of the law that the 2013 Supreme Court decision killed, but getting these types of legislative proposals past current Senate Majority Leader Mitch McConnell is exceedingly difficult and unlikely.) So shenanigans that limit voters' access to the polls have roared back into our electoral system.

Now before we get further into this discussion, let's make one thing clear: we each have to make our own "policy" call when it comes to the debate around laws that make voting harder. A policy call means that we each have to decide which of the competing concerns and objectives regarding voting, on balance, matter to us most in this debate. On one hand, there's the argument outlined previously—that carrying identification is a routine fact of life. In many states, having a valid driver's license is all that you need to vote. What's the hassle, then, with imposing requirements on voting?

On the other hand, we've just spent a lot of time talking about things like dark money in politics, and how the Electoral College and political gerrymandering create major disconnects between the votes cast by individuals and the policies actually made by those in power. If we are a government by "We the People," we must stand together with other individuals and demand that our voices be the ones collectively calling the shots—not the voices of the politicians already in power.

The alternative is power entrenched in the already powerful—not more power for regular people over the long run. On balance, then, perhaps we can agree that more access to voting for a greater number of individuals is better for everyone as a whole than keeping people from the polls to secure the power of the already powerful. The risk of a few "wrong" people voting, in other words, is worth the reward: democracy by the people.

Keep in mind that criminal penalties for voter fraud already exist to the tune of $5,000 and five years in prison.[3] The possibility of going to jail may be enough disincentive to ensure that people do the right thing and vote honestly. The upside to illegally voting and risking a criminal violation is teeny. A person who breaks those laws only gets, in exchange, to cast a single vote in an election—she certainly can't sway the whole thing. It's just not worth the risk of prison.

The debate comes down to "access" versus "integrity." In the end, it depends on people's media diet. Some people hear about eligible voters being turned away and become worried about voter suppression. Other people hear that people who shouldn't be voting are voting and so they back rules protecting vote integrity. If you agree that we might at least consider erring on the side of opening—versus closing—the voting tent, then the next question becomes: What's actually happening on the ground out there? Is voter suppression really a problem? Are legitimate voters arbitrarily being kept from voting?

On the flip side, are the criminal laws against voter fraud not working? Do we need more barriers erected—that is, stricter registration and voting requirements—to ensure that those willing to take the risk of a criminal infraction don't succeed because it's also too hard to get to the ballot box in the first place? Let's take up these issues one by one.

Voter Suppression

In 2018, Democrat Stacey Abrams ran for governor of Georgia. She was the first African American woman in the history of the United States to top the gubernatorial ticket for a major political party. Her opponent, Brian Kemp, was Georgia's secretary of state at the time. Kemp ultimately won the election by 1.4 percentage points.[4]

Many of us have heard of Abrams and might even recall the hullabaloo surrounding that race. The reason it was such a big deal was that, as secretary of state, Kemp was also the *chief elections official* for the state of Georgia. That's right. He was both running for office and deciding the rules of the game at the same time. As a matter of human nature, how many of us wouldn't do what we could to skew an election in our favor if we held the power to do so? Imagine an umpire in a kids' baseball game. Team Green is playing Team Purple. The umpire's kid is on Team Green. The stakes are high—the winning team goes to the national championships. If the umpire is handed the authority to tweak the actual rules of the game as it goes along, let's face it: Team Purple may be at a disadvantage.

In Georgia, the secretary of state coordinates and monitors voter registration. He manages all municipal, state, county, and federal elections. He oversees compliance with the state's campaign finance disclosure rules for state and federal candidates, as well as for PACs. He is responsible for investigating and enforcing state laws against voter fraud. He certifies candidates as qualified to run for office. He prepares the ballots and other election forms. He maintains a statewide voter registration list. And he certifies the results of elections—that is, he declares the winners. For his part, with ballots still being counted, Kemp resigned his position as secretary of state two days after declaring victory in the campaign for governor.[5]

What did Kemp do with his referee power that might have helped his bid for the highest office in the state? Well, Kemp served as Georgia's secretary of state from 2010 to 2018. A lawsuit filed in November 2018 set forth a menu of things that Kemp allegedly did to help himself win the governorship. The plaintiffs claimed that, according to "[t]he U.S. Commission on Civil Rights, a bipartisan, independent agency," Georgia had implemented "strict requirements for voter identification; documentary proof of U.S. citizenship; purges of voters from voter registration rolls; cuts to early voting; and a raft of closed or relocated polling locations" keeping legitimate voters from the polls.[6] And "[w]ithout the right to vote," the plaintiffs quipped, "all other democratic rights are illusory. Fair elections ensure the consent of the governed; they are the moral foundation of the compact between the government and its citizens."[7]

Some well-meaning Georgia voters unwittingly bumped up

against Kemp's "exact match" registration verification process. Under that program, voter registrations that did not precisely match state drivers' license or Social Security records were placed on hold. So, for example, if you put your middle initial down in registering to vote but used your full middle name in applying for a driver's license, you could be cut from the polls—without even knowing it. Under Kemp, 54,000 registrations were put on hold and 107,000 people were taken off Georgia's voter registration lists altogether prior to the 2018 election.[8] Regardless of your residence or political party affiliation, the moral of this story is this: you should care—a lot—about these kinds of shenanigans, because if left unchecked, you could one day wind up very frustrated and even angry on Election Day. Having placed 54,000 registrations on hold for failing the exact match rule, Kemp went on to win the 2018 election by 54,723 votes. Bingo.[9]

The Supreme Court is partly to blame for the states' new restrictions on voting. Recall again that in 1965, Congress passed the Voting Rights Act, which was aimed at disrupting state efforts to discourage or prevent people from voting. In 2013, the Supreme Court struck down an important part of that statute requiring that certain states and local governments get a "thumbs-up" from the federal government before changing their voting practices. Congress had determined that racial discrimination was simply too entrenched in many states, known as "covered jurisdictions." The law contained a formula for determining which states and local governments needed a thumbs-up by the federal government before they could impose new voting procedures (called "preclearance"). The legislation put a check on states' ability to impose onerous conditions on voting or registering to vote.

In a case named *Shelby County v. Holder*, the Supreme Court by a 5–4 vote struck down the statute's mathematical formula for deciding which states were covered jurisdictions—all while acknowledging the "serious and widespread intentional discrimination [that] persisted in covered jurisdictions."[10] States can now change their voting laws without running the proposed changes by DOJ. In the lawsuit challenging Kemp's gubernatorial victory in Georgia, the plaintiffs alleged that it was after *Shelby* that "Georgia began again to erect discriminatory voting barriers reminiscent of the Jim Crow era."

The Kemp team's rationale for the exact match rule was that voters need to be verified to prevent fraud—a rationale used by politicians across the country to justify adding new hurdles to voting.[11] But again, we each have to make a policy call here. Ensuring that only the right people vote is an important objective, for sure. "We the People" should only include eligible voters who follow the voting laws—not ineligible people who violate the laws against voter fraud. But we also know that voting is central to our entire constitutional system. We don't have a monarchy in America. The bosses of our government are the people. An overpowerful government must be avoided, because it would allow those in power to take actions against regular people based on arbitrary criteria—such as a target's political point of view. It's vital that we keep the power in the people. Restrictions on the ability to exercise that power strike at the core of our freedoms. We should be very, very careful about condoning them.

So let's get back to a key question: Is voter fraud a serious enough threat to the integrity of our voting process to keep legitimate voters from the polls? As we will see, the facts show that the answer is no. The framers of the Constitution fully understood that voting is unlikely to kill democracy. They instead believed that the malignancy for democracy would be too much power amassed in the hands of those already in power. They were right.

Voter Fraud

There are, of course, many pressing problems—even crises—that politicians and regular people are dealing with every day. The data shows that confronting voter fraud is not one of them. You are more likely to be struck by lightning or devoured by a shark than have a fraudulent voter darken your precinct's door. The fact that voter fraud is no big deal makes logical sense. Why? Because criminal laws put you in prison for five years if you cast a fake vote. With nothing to be gained by fraudulently voting, people have no incentive to do it—and ample incentive not to.

Some worry that voter fraud exists on a wide scale even if there is no evidence to prove it. But it's worth taking a pause and consulting our common sense about what a fact of evidence means. We do know more than a few things as established facts, however. The earth is orbiting around the sun, grass is green, and water is wet. Empirical facts are real. Science depends on them. Facts are why we have lifesaving medicines and massive bridges that don't routinely crumble beneath us and satellites in space. Smoking causes cancer, and seat belts save lives. Pair a single apple and a single pear and you get two pieces of fruit. And so on. Facts are real and they are important.

When it comes to voter fraud, here are the facts: It's exceedingly rare. It happens between 0.0003 percent and 0.0025 percent of the time. Out of one billion votes cast from 2000 to 2014, research revealed a paltry thirty-one instances of voters casting fraudulent votes in person. It almost never happens. Most problems with improper voting stem from clerical and computer errors. According to scholars affiliated with Stanford University, the University of Pennsylvania, Harvard University, and Yale University, during the 2012 election cycle, the possibility that a registered voter would commit fraud by voting twice was under 0.02 percent.[12] Fraud is more likely to be committed by campaigns engaging in fraudulent voter registrations or fraudulent absentee ballot applications or submissions.[13]

Compare these statistics with the facts bearing on the other side of the coin: new voting restrictions that make it harder for legitimate voters to vote. Since 2010, twenty-five states have enacted measures that include strict photo requirements, cutbacks on early and absentee voting opportunities, and restrictions on the ability to register and stay registered.[14] Many states enacted these kinds of laws in just the past couple of years. According to data from the federal government, over twelve thousand physical polling sites were closed from 2008 to 2016. Other states have cut back on polling staff. Closed or relocated polling places and fewer poll workers mean longer lines. If it's harder for people to get to the polls in a timely manner on Election Day, people can't vote—even if they desperately want to.

Studies also show that the people most affected by these new restrictions are those living in precincts with a higher percentage of low-income and minority voters. Remember that it's human nature for people in power to amass and entrench their power. Opening the polls to minority voters is a threat to certain politicians' hold on power, so it's no surprise that after the *Shelby County* case, these attempts to outmaneuver voters have popped up again.[15]

There are still ways to alleviate barriers to voting. Congress could, of course, fix the Voting Rights Act to please the Supreme Court. (As I noted previously, the Democratic-controlled House has passed a bill to do this. If you think it's a good idea, call your senators and urge them to move it in the Senate too.) For an everyday person, the first step to addressing problems with voting in America is easy: accept the facts as they exist—that is, that voter fraud is largely a myth, and that we need to be circumspect about going too far in erecting barriers to voting. While we must do everything we can to ensure the integrity of our elections and people's faith in electoral outcomes, draconian registration and voting laws are like fixing a splinter with an amputation. We don't need them, and they come at a high price. The second step, then, might be to insist that elected officials lift existing restrictions on voting, but that's hardly realistic, either—particularly given that restrictions are on the rise since 2010.

The third possible step relies again on Congress. We might tolerate state-specific restrictions on voting, but agree, as a nation, not to have our election system run by partisans from one party or another who are incentivized to manipulate the rules for their own benefit. Neutral, voter-focused commissions might produce rules and procedures that benefit the populace as a whole without gaming the system one way or another.

The fourth—and perhaps most promising—pathway to alleviating barriers to voting is for eligible voters to educate themselves regarding what they need to do to register, to maintain their registration, and to vote. And then *do those things.* That's a steep climb, for many. People are cynical about voting, and might just stay home in "protest." Or because there are more important ways to spend one's time. But doing nothing does, well, nothing. American democracy is a gift. Not everyone on the planet has the power to govern themselves and to throw out leaders that might abuse power and hurt regular people. If you're reading or listening to this book, you've already taken this fourth step toward protecting your own democracy. When you've finished the book, the next step is to pass the information along to the next person, so that others can become educated on the pathways to voting too.

DISCUSSION QUESTIONS FOR CHAPTER 11

- Were you surprised to learn that voter fraud is a myth? Why do you think the belief in its existence is so widespread? Do you see a tension lurking here between the desires of politicians and the will of the people?

- What does *Shelby County v. Holder* suggest about the power of the US Supreme Court—or, more accurately, the power of five justices in the majority? Recall that a piece of legislation, in theory, reflects the will of the people. Unlike federal judges, members of Congress are elected. The Voting Rights Act was repeatedly renewed with overwhelming bipartisan support. Is there an argument that the Supreme Court should be very cautious about overturning such a law?

- How are you feeling after reading this chapter? Anxious? Emboldened? What's one thing you might change in your own life as a result of the knowledge you just gained?

12

Voter Misinformation: A Primer on Foreign Interference in US Presidential Elections

Chapter 12 Takeaway Box

- Election interference happens two primary ways: cyberattacks and duping voters with misinformation.

- US national security officials have concluded that the Russians did both in the 2016 presidential election, and that it is happening again for 2020.
- Democracies in Europe have been attacked too, and it's not just Russia doing the attacking.
- Regardless of one's political party affiliation, these kinds of attacks are a serious problem for American democracy and the ability of regular voters to govern themselves.

For decades to come, historians will analyze and debate the importance and impact of Special Counsel Robert Mueller's investigation of Russian interference in the 2016 presidential election as well as the narrative that led to President Trump's impeachment: his pressuring of Ukraine to announce an investigation of Joe Biden in exchange for Senate-approved military aid that Ukraine needed to fight the Russians and hold on to democracy. Thus far, at least anecdotally, these stories appear to have had at least one very unfortunate effect: some voters believe more than ever that the electoral process is so overtaken by foreign influence that it's hardly worth bothering to go to the polls. This is deeply disheartening. Unfortunately, candidates have not figured out a way to talk about this type of interference without making voters feel that the whole process is so distorted that voting is not worth it.

As we discussed in the last chapter, although this view is understandable, it's extremely unfortunate—and probably counterproductive to the interests of regular voters and their families. Staying home from the polls plays into the hands of outside forces seeking to control

American politics. A vibrant system of voting is the primary means by which politicians are held accountable by regular people. Doing nothing to participate in that process, again, does nothing. That's not to say that a single vote will change the course of American politics. It won't. But if votes didn't matter, politicians and adverse foreign governments wouldn't work so hard to influence how—and whether—people vote.

Russia's attack on the 2016 presidential election is the most recent and prominent example of how foreign governments, extremist groups, or even single individuals use cyberattacks and social media to influence elections in the United States. Such efforts did not start with the 2016 election, however. In 2012, for example, China tried to infiltrate the servers of Mitt Romney's campaign for president. Such attacks aren't confined to US elections, either. They also occur in European democracies. Back in 1974, the Soviet KGB waged a covert misinformation campaign in France to discredit certain politicians in favor of others. France took active measures in response, which worked to hamper Russia's attempts to interfere in France's presidential election again in 2017.

Keep in mind that foreign governments' objective is not to help everyday American voters get their needs heard and addressed by their elected officials. Far from it. Regardless of one's political party, foreign interference in elections is bad, bad, bad for us. In 2016, the attacks happened to favor Donald Trump, who went on to win the presidency. But that's really beside the point. As Mitt Romney's former campaign manager noted, "cyberattacks are a bipartisan problem requiring cross-party solutions." Although he and Hillary Clinton's 2016 campaign manager "don't agree on much politically," he added, "one thing we are in lockstep on is that only U.S. voters should decide U.S. elections."[1]

Recall again the kids' baseball game analogy. If the umpire is being paid off or threatened by Purple Team supporters, he might call the game for the Purple Team no matter how well the Green Team plays. If that happens, it's not even a game anymore. It's a predetermined win for Purple. The Green Team parents will get angry. They might even pull their kids out of the league entirely. It's just no fun if, on any particular day, the game is stacked in favor of one team over the other.

Foreign governments seeking to undermine American democracy know this. They want people to decide not to participate. As David Becker of the Center for Election Innovation and Research explained, "They don't necessarily need to change the outcome of races or change voter records. What they can do is attack our systems and get us to delegitimize our own democracy." They get us to turn against ourselves. So, again, let's not take that bait—go ahead and exercise your vote.

As far as we know, there are two primary tactics used to infiltrate democratic elections: cyberattacks and social media agitation aimed at duping people into voting a certain way—or into not voting at all.[2] Let's break those things down a bit more.

Cyberattacks

Cyberattacks on electoral systems can take a number of forms. Tactics include:

- **Denial-of-service** (DoS) attacks, which shut down networks and make it difficult or impossible for legitimate users to access information systems. Commonly, an attacker will overload a network server with illegitimate digital traffic and fake return addresses. The server gets confused when it tries to authenticate the source of the requests. It becomes overwhelmed and inaccessible to regular users. Attackers can also go after a network's internet service provider (ISP) or cloud service provider, which will ricochet throughout the networks served by the ISP, causing them to lose service. In a "distributed" DoS attack, multiple machines attack one target at the same time, allowing exponentially more requests to be sent to the server or ISP and making it much harder to identify the source of the attack. This kind of DoS attack often uses a "botnet"—which hijacks and infects a bunch of individual devices connected to the internet all at once, using command-and-control software. The hijacked devices conduct the DoS attack unwittingly and are also victims of the scheme. Once the botnet is created, it may be rented out to other would-be attackers. This type of attack was used against states in 2016, flooding online voter registration systems with requests and effectively shutting out legitimate citizens who were attempting to register.[3]

- **Phishing** is exactly what it sounds like—the attacker throws the victim some bait and hopes he will bite. In the case of cyberphishing, the bait is an email that appears in a person's in-box under the pretense that it's legitimate. The email could look like an urgent request from the IRS or a bank or even a benign note from a colleague. The email will ask the user to click on an attachment or a malicious URL. Once the user clicks, the user's computer gets infected with **malware**—also known as viruses or worms—that allow attackers to steal personal information or login credentials. In 2016, a phishing attack allowed Russian hackers to get the Gmail password of Hillary Clinton campaign chair John Podesta. Podesta thought the phishing email was a real email sent by Google telling him that someone had used his password to try to sign into his Gmail account. It added: "Google stopped this sign-in attempt. You should change your password immediately" and included a link to change his password. Whoever changed Podesta's password clicked on a fake URL that allowed Russian hackers to steal Podesta's emails. They were released by the thousands by WikiLeaks in the days leading up the 2016 presidential election.[4]

- **Ransomware** attacks are a form of malware, which, as noted earlier, infects a computer with a virus by allowing it to piggyback on a document or hide in a fake URL. The malware steals information, deletes or corrupts files, and/or reconfigures the computer's hardware. Malware can spread to other computers too. Ransomware is a form of malware in which the attacker notifies the user's system that it has been attacked—but only after it has done something to corrupt the computer. The notification demands some sort of payment, usually in cryptocurrency, to restore the computer to its prior state remotely. Even when ransomware attackers are paid, they do not always readjust the system as promised. Russian hackers used malware on voter registration systems in 2016. The Department of Homeland Security's Cybersecurity Infrastructure Security Agency, or CISA, is worried that foreign hackers will target voter databases in 2020 to manipulate or destroy data used to validate voter eligibility. One senior official said that the systems are potential "targets for ransomware attacks" that are assessed "as high risk." States and municipalities need to secure their websites and databases, but currently no federal guidelines exist to help states determine whether they should pay ransom to hackers if a voting system becomes infected. In response to the Russian attacks in 2016, some—but not all—state and local governments have created backups in case the data is compromised.[5] These efforts also cost money that states might not have or might decide to spend on other priorities.

A final question on many people's minds is this: Were any votes actually changed as a result of Russian interference in the 2016 elections? Because if not, should we even care about Russian interference in the 2016 election?

The question is important for one obvious reason: Democratic candidate Hillary Clinton lost the critical swing states of Michigan, Pennsylvania, and Wisconsin by fewer than eighty thousand total votes—thus losing the Electoral College and the election, even though she won nearly four times more total votes overall.[6] Did the Russians' meddling actually add to Trump's eighty-thousand-vote margin?

Probably not. Although a Report of the Senate Select Committee on Intelligence concluded that Russian attacks on US election infrastructure were "extensive" from at least 2014 to at least 2017, it saw "no evidence that any votes were changed or that any voting machines were manipulated."[7]

Social Media Agitation

The second way that attackers try to interfere in elections is by stoking agitation on social media. The framers of the Constitution decided to create a republic—whereby individuals have their voices heard through representatives in Congress, not by counting up votes—instead of a direct democracy because they knew that it's human nature for people to divide into "factions," or polarized groups. Dividing people from the inside out against each other is an effective way to make sure that nothing gets done in a democracy, which requires compromise. The framers also knew that factions that are ideologically motivated can become inflamed by propaganda—information that triggers an emotional response but does not necessarily produce policy outcomes that are good for the country as a whole.[8]

Teenagers know a few things about this phenomenon. It's impossible to get through high school without having to deal with rumors. Once gossip gets on the grapevine, it quickly devolves into something far afield from the actual truth, and people get hurt in the process. If a rumor is about someone from the popular girl "clique," for example, others who feel marginalized by the clique might glom onto the gossip more than an objective outsider, who might be quite skeptical of it. What "team" we feel we are on, in other words, can dictate how much credence we give to a rumor about a particular politician on the internet.

History shows that rumors can have serious consequences on a national scale. In the fourteenth century, rumors spread that Jews were poisoning the wells of Christians in exchange for Satan's protection from the Black Plague. Thousands of Jews were killed or expelled as a consequence. On the eve of the French Revolution in July 1789, rumors spread that the nobles had hired robbers to terrorize the peasants and steal their food. Villages and towns formed militias in fear, but no robbers showed up. The story was fabricated. In 1914, three years before the United States entered World War I, rumors spread that German Americans were planning stealth invasions in Canada and had begun drilling in Niagara Falls and Buffalo, New York. Unlike the United States, Canada had already entered the war. The Canadian prime minister was sufficiently concerned to order a report on the invasion rumor, which turned out to be false. Most recently, in April 2013, a fake tweet circulated from a hacked Associated Press account stating that President Obama had been injured by explosions at the White House. In response, a stock index plunged $130 billion, recovering quickly once it was clear that the rumor was false.[9]

Hackers understand that rumors can affect how people vote, so they use them, too, to sway elections. Here are a few methods that hackers use to do it:

- **Shame publications** are releases of information obtained illegally with the intent of exposing or embarrassing someone. This is what happened in 2016 with WikiLeaks's release of John Podesta's emails relating to the Clinton campaign.
- **False fronts** involve the fabrication of a completely false identity—a fake person on Facebook, Twitter, or Instagram—who spreads messages that the attacker wants people to think are coming from a real person. False fronts are often used to amplify particular sentiments for

or against a candidate or party. In 2016, for example, the Russians created the persona of a fake person they named Melvin Redick of Harrisburg, Pennsylvania. He was friendly-looking, wore a backward baseball cap, and had a fake daughter. He posted a link on his Facebook page with the message: "These guys show hidden truth about Hillary Clinton, George Soros and other leaders of the US. Visit #DCLeaks website. It's really interesting!" The link was controlled by Russians. Facebook later shut down hundreds of sites they believed were created by a Russian company with links to Russian president Vladimir Putin. On Twitter, there are hundreds or thousands of such fake accounts that employ bots—or web robots—to send out automated political hashtags to unsuspecting users at an exponentially higher rate than live humans could achieve. Twitter has approximately 330 million users who can be affected by these scams. Facebook has nearly two billion. You do the math.[10]

- **Fabricated content** is, well, making up false information and spreading it as if it were true. This can come in the form of false information about a candidate, or by spreading false data. Imagine news that exit polls reveal a landslide for Candidate X. It's a lie. But people who might have gone out to vote for Candidate Y don't know that. They decide to stay home, and Candidate X wins the election. Attackers can plant all kinds of information designed to dissuade voters from showing up at the polls and voting for the opposing candidate. Technology has also developed that allows attackers to create "deep fakes," which are videos of avatars stating false or even incriminating things. The deep fakes look like real people, so viewers don't know if the real people actually said what the videos reflect them saying. A politician who is targeted by a deep fake might get on air to deny he said what the avatar said, but how does he prove to viewers that the second video is the real one? As voters in the digital age, how do we know what to believe? This is a serious problem, and those wishing to hijack our electoral process know it.[11]

Is Congress Doing Anything?

Some people reading this chapter might discount it as its own form of false propaganda. Special Counsel Robert Mueller and others concluded that the Russians' interference favored Trump in 2016, not Hillary Clinton. If you happen to support Trump for president in 2020, you might look askance at any discussion of election meddling designed to help his campaign.

But recall our discussion about what it means to make decisions based on facts. We can acknowledge a fact exists and still decide that it's not worth doing anything about that fact. That's very different from denying the existence of the fact in the first place. Some people accept the fact that there are billions of germs on the doorknobs of public restrooms, but they decide to open the door with a bare hand anyway. Others accept that same fact and choose to use a tissue or paper towel to open the door so that they can avoid the germs. When it comes to foreign interference, we can accept the fact that it happens and that it will continue to happen and decide to do nothing.

Or we can accept the fact and decide that—regardless of which candidates it might help or hurt in a particular election cycle—we don't want to be duped or lied to by foreigners or other bad actors intent on distorting American elections, and we certainly don't want to make important decisions about whom to vote for based on lies. Even if we like today's winner and aren't bothered that she may have been helped by voter manipulation efforts, we might dislike tomorrow's winner and be very upset that he may have been helped by voter manipulation efforts. Why not clear out the lies planted by foreign governments and anti-democracy influencers and vote for our candidates based on the actual facts? There's no harm—and only benefit—in that, right?

So what has Congress done—if anything—about these endemic problems? The short answer is that Congress has done a bit, but not enough. In 2018, Congress passed legislation providing $380 million in grants for states to use in addressing the security of their election systems. Some people say the amount is insufficient to meet the severity of the need. Beyond that, not much has been done at the federal level. People in Congress have introduced legislation to address election security, in particular, but Republicans under Senate Majority Leader Mitch McConnell blocked election-security legislation from reaching the Senate floor.[12]

Nonetheless, the Department of Homeland Security and state election administrators have been working tirelessly to coordinate and develop best practices to ensure that elections are secure.[13] Recall that the federal government doesn't administer elections—states do. And many states would prefer that Congress not get involved. After all, it's much harder to hack fifty-one (this number includes the District of Columbia) separate state election systems—and approximately ten thousand local ones—than a single federal one.

Federal funding for new and updated voting systems—which the states can choose and administer for themselves—remains critical. State budgets may be understandably challenged by the expense of purchasing new voting systems. The need for updated election equipment may be outweighed by other important priorities like public safety, education, and health care. With support from DHS, the FBI, and other federal agencies, a huge amount is being done by the states to shore up electoral integrity by, for example, keeping voter registration databases from becoming infected with ransomware.[14] Such efforts are absolutely vital to sustaining and ensuring a government by "We the People." I, for one, am grateful for them.

DISCUSSION QUESTIONS FOR CHAPTER 12

- Do you think Congress should do more about foreign interference in our elections? If not, why not? If yes, what should be done?

- What does congressional inaction on this issue have to say about the functioning of our federal legislature? If not Congress, who should address these problems and why?

- How much has modern technology come into play in the discussion over the security of our elections? How has technology affected your own life? Do you have concerns for the security of your own personal data that help give perspective on how and why outsiders attempt to attack our electoral systems?

Conclusion

In setting up the duties of the federal government and the coordinate rights of "We the People," the framers of the Constitution did many things right and arguably they did many things wrong. One thing they didn't do is enshrine a constitutional right to vote in the original text. We have rights to free speech and to a jury trial in criminal cases—but not a textual right to vote. Yet voting remains the core mechanism by which we govern ourselves. Why is it even a topic of debate these days?

In 1788, the only people who mattered for self-government were property-owning white men. Since then the constitutional text has dramatically changed to incorporate people of all races and genders by forbidding the government from denying them the franchise. But the United States remains a patchwork of voting systems, requirements, and mechanisms. That patchwork makes it impossible to achieve "equal" voting rights across the nation. Although we no longer have categorical denials of the right to vote, we still have problems with voter access and election integrity—as well as a sharp, pragmatic disconnect between the needs and desires of the voting public and the policies that wind up actually implemented by our elected officials.

People want to know two things: What can be done about these problems? And perhaps even more perniciously, given these problems, why should we bother to vote in the first place?

If you take nothing else away from this book, I hope you take away the importance and privilege of being able to participate in free elections, however imperfect they may be. Think about what it would be like to live instead in a country where your vote really didn't matter. Where the people with the power of the military, the police, and the courts at their fingertips don't care what you think—because the system doesn't make them care. Many people on this planet live under such regimes and can only dream about the voting rights that Americans enjoy.

Remember the framers knew one thing about human psychology: it's in our nature to amass, entrench, and ultimately abuse power. The structure of the government needs checks and balances in place to stave off such abuses. We all know this from daily life. Our places of work, places of worship, and living spaces all have written, spoken, or unspoken rules of conduct that exist to make the systems work. If the rules aren't enforced, chaos resumes. If restaurant workers can steal from the cash register without consequence, for example, the restaurant will close. The same goes for a government that's accountable to the people. The Constitution is just a piece of paper—if it's not enforced at the ballot booth, it has no real meaning for how we live in relationship to people with political power.

In our system of democracy, the key mechanism for enforcing the constitutional and legal rules governing our elected officials is voting. To be able to cast a ballot in the United States is nothing short of a gift and a privilege—even if you feel that one ballot cast won't make a difference in the moment. Honoring that privilege is to honor those who fought and died for it, and to preserve it for our children and grandchildren who do not have the ability to go to the polls and exercise the rights of American democracy today.

Remember, too, that state legislatures remain accountable to their voters for how they decide to implement and administer federal, state, and local elections. If you care about how voting works, lobby your elected officials and cast your vote in ways that might change the system. It's the only way to fix things in America—and it's so, so worth it.

Acknowledgments

The author wishes to thank, first and foremost, Sara Nelson—an exceptional editor and mentor, who understood immediately the importance of broadening legal literacy beyond the law school classroom. It's been a great pleasure and honor to work with Sara on this book as well as on my prior work, *How to Read the Constitution—and Why*. Thanks, too, to my agent, Paul Fedorko, whose great wisdom, experience, and cheerful demeanor has made this experience a real joy. I also want to thank Mary Gaule and everyone else at HarperCollins who met tight deadlines to get this book on the shelves in advance of the 2020 election. My wonderful friends and colleagues Alexandra Stoddard, Amanda LaForge, Ann Jablon, and Gayraud Townsend all shared valuable substantive expertise—many thanks to them (any mistakes are mine, of course). Adeen Postar, Dave Matchen, Raquel Flynn, Sarah Hernandez, Curtis Paul, Calvin Riorda, and Amanda Scanlon provided superb research and citation support. Thanks, too, to my assistant at the University of Baltimore, Debbie Pinkham, for enthusiastically picking up whatever tasks come her way, and to Penny Ross Burk for her beautiful and brilliant illustrations. Finally, I want to thank my intern, Cat Scott, who has been the engine behind my social media presence, a vital tool for getting the message out on the importance of the rule of law in America.

Appendix

State-by-State Registration Requirements

STATE	DEADLINE TO REGISTER TO VOTE	WHERE AND HOW TO REGISTER
Alabama	In person: 15 days before Election Day By mail: Postmarked 15 days before Election Day Online: 15 days before Election Day	In person: Local board of registrars or any office providing public assistance By mail: Office of the Secretary of State P.O. Box 5616 Montgomery, AL 36103–5616
Alaska	In person: 30 days before Election Day By mail: Postmarked 30 days before Election Day Online: 30 days before Election Day	In person: Local board of registrars or any office providing public assistance By mail: Region I Elections Office PO Box 110018 Juneau, AK 998811–0018 Online: https://voterregistration.alaska.gov
Arizona	In person: 29 days before Election Day By mail: Postmarked 29 days before Election Day Online: 29 days before Election Day	In person: Local board of registrars or any office providing public assistance By mail: Mail to your county's County Recorder office Online: https://servicearizona.com/voter Registration
Arkansas	In person: 30 days before Election Day By mail: Postmarked 30 days before Election Day	In person: Local county clerk's office By mail: Local county clerk's office

WHERE TO FIND INFORMATION ON THE CANDIDATES	PRIMARY OR CAUCUS? OPEN OR CLOSED?	MAIL-IN VOTING?
https://www.sos.alabama.gov/alabama-votes/voter/election-information	Open primary	Yes, for absentee ballots
http://www.elections.alaska.gov/Core/candidateinformation.php	Partially closed system. Each party may allow unaffiliated voters to participate. However, this does not apply to presidential elections.	Yes, for absentee ballots
https://azsos.gov/elections	Open primary	Yes, for absentee ballots
https://www.sos.arkansas.gov/elections/information-for-candidates	Open primary	Yes, for absentee ballots

STATE	DEADLINE TO REGISTER TO VOTE	WHERE AND HOW TO REGISTER
California	In person: 15 days before Election Day By mail: Postmarked 15 days before Election Day Online: 15 days before Election Day	In person: Local county election's office By mail: Mail to your local county election's office Online: https://registertovote.ca.gov
Colorado	In person: On Election Day By mail: Received 8 days before Election Day Online: 8 days before Election Day	In person: Local board of registrars or any office providing public assistance By mail: Mail to your county's County Recorder office Online: https://www.sos.state.co.us/pubs/elections/vote/VoterHome.html
Connecticut	In person: 7 days before Election Day By mail: Postmarked 7 days before Election Day Online: 7 days before Election Day	In person: Local board of registrars or any office providing public assistance By mail: Mail to your county's County Recorder office Online: https://voterregistration.ct.gov/OLVR/welcome.do
Delaware	In person: 24 days before Election Day By mail: Postmarked 24 days before Election Day Online: 24 days before Election Day	In person: Local board of registrars or any office providing public assistance By mail: Mail to your county's County Recorder office Online: https://elections.delaware.gov/services/voter/placestoregister.shtml
District of Columbia	In person: On Election Day, with proof of residency By mail: Received 21 days before Election Day Online: 21 days before Election Day	In person: DC Board of Elections Office, DMV, polling place By mail: DC Board of Elections Office, DMV, polling place Online: https://www.vote4dc.com/ApplyInstructions/Register

WHERE TO FIND INFORMATION ON THE CANDIDATES	PRIMARY OR CAUCUS? OPEN OR CLOSED?	MAIL-IN VOTING?
https://www.sos.ca.gov/elections/upcoming-elections/candidate-information/	Closed primary There is also a "top-two" primary system wherein the top-two vote-getters advance to the general election regardless of party for state or local primaries.	Yes, for absentee ballots
https://www.sos.state.co.us/pubs/elections/electionInfo.html	Semiclosed primary open to unaffiliated voters.	Yes, it is allowed
https://portal.ct.gov/SOTS/Election-Services/V5-Side-Navigation/ELECandidate-Information	Closed primary	Yes, for absentee ballots
https://elections.delaware.gov/services/candidate/candidate_list.shtml	Closed primary	Yes, for absentee ballots
https://www.dcboe.org/#	Closed primary	Yes, for absentee ballots

STATE	DEADLINE TO REGISTER TO VOTE	WHERE AND HOW TO REGISTER
Florida	In person: 29 days before Election Day By mail: Postmarked 29 days before Election Day Online: 29 days before Election Day	In person: local board of registrars or any office providing public assistance By mail: Mail to your county's County Recorder office Online: https://registertovoteflorida.gov/en/Registration/Index
Georgia	In person: 29 days before Election Day By mail: Postmarked 29 days before Election Day Online: 29 days before Election Day	In person: Local board of registrars or any office providing public assistance By mail: Mail to your county's county board of registrar's office Online: https://sos.ga.gov/index.php/Elections/register_to_vote
Hawaii	In person: 29 days before Election Day By mail: Received 29 days before Election Day Online: 29 days before Election Day	In person: Local clerk's office By mail: Mail to your local clerk's office Online: https://olvr.hawaii.gov
Idaho	In person: Election day, with proof of residency By mail: Postmarked 25 days before Election Day Online: 25 days before Election Day	In person: Local board of registrars or any office providing public assistance By mail: Mail to your county's County Recorder office Online: https://apps.idahovotes.gov/OnlineVoterRegistration
Illinois	In person: Election Day By mail: Postmarked 28 days before Election Day Online: 16 days before Election Day	In person: Local board of registrars or any office providing public assistance By mail: Mail to your county's County Recorder office Online: https://ova.elections.il.gov

WHERE TO FIND INFORMATION ON THE CANDIDATES	PRIMARY OR CAUCUS? OPEN OR CLOSED?	MAIL-IN VOTING?
https://dos.myflorida.com/elections/candidates-committees/information-about-candidates-campaign-documents-and-committees/	Closed primary	Yes, for absentee ballots
https://elections.sos.ga.gov/GAElection/CandidateDetails	Open primary	Yes, for absentee ballots
https://elections.hawaii.gov	Closed caucus (R) Closed primary (D)	Yes, for all voters
https://idahovotes.gov/candidate-information-directory/	Closed primary (R) Semiclosed primary (D)	Yes, for absentee ballots
https://elections.suntimes.com/voting-guide/2020/	Semi-open primary	Yes, for absentee ballots

STATE	DEADLINE TO REGISTER TO VOTE	WHERE AND HOW TO REGISTER
Indiana	In person: 29 days before Election Day By mail: Postmarked 29 days before Election Day Online: 29 days before Election Day	In person: Voter registration office or office of election division By mail: Mail to your county's voter registration office or office of election division Online: https://votesmart.org/election/2018/S/IL/2018-statewide#.XSviUy2ZNQI
Iowa	In person: 10 days before Election Day, or on Election Day By mail: Postmarked 15 days before Election Day or received 10 days before Election Day Online: 10 days before Election Day	In person: At the polling place or election division office By mail: Mail to your county's voter registration office or office of election division Online: https://sos.iowa.gov/elections/voterinformation/voterregistration.html
Kansas	In person: 21 days before Election Day By mail: Postmarked 21 days before Election Day Online: 21 days before Election Day	In person: Voter registration office or office of election division By mail: Mail to your county's voter registration office or office of election division Online: https://www.kdor.ks.gov/apps/voterreg/default.aspx
Kentucky	In person: 29 days before Election Day By mail: Postmarked 29 days before Election Day Online: 29 days before Election Day	In person: Voter registration office or state board of elections By mail: Mail to State Board of Elections Online: https://vrsws.sos.ky.gov/ovrweb/

WHERE TO FIND INFORMATION ON THE CANDIDATES	PRIMARY OR CAUCUS? OPEN OR CLOSED?	MAIL-IN VOTING?
https://www.in.gov/sos/elections/2395.htm	Semi-open primary	Yes, for absentee ballots
https://sos.iowa.gov/elections/voterinformation/voterregistration.html	Caucus	Yes, for absentee ballots
https://uselections.com/ks/ks.htm	Closed caucus	Yes, for absentee ballots
http://votekentucky.us	Closed primary	Yes, for absentee ballots

STATE	DEADLINE TO REGISTER TO VOTE	WHERE AND HOW TO REGISTER
Louisiana	In person: 30 days before Election Day By mail: Received 30 days before Election Day Online: 20 days before Election Day	In person: Any registrar of voters office, DMV, or public assistance offices By mail: Mail to your local registrar of voters office Online: https://voterportal.sos.la.gov/VoterRegistration
Maine	In person: Election Day By mail: Received 21 days before Election Day	In person: Town office, city hall, or motor vehicle branch office By mail: Mail to secretary of state's office in Augusta
Maryland	In person: 5 days before Election Day By mail: Postmarked 21 days before Election Day Online: 21 days before Election Day	In person: Voter registration office or local board of elections By mail: Mail to your local board of elections Online: https://voterservices.elections.maryland.gov/OnlineVoterRegistration/VoterType
Massachusetts	In person: 20 days before Election Day By mail: Postmarked 20 days before Election Day Online: 20 days before Election Day	In person: Any local election office, elections division office, or motor vehicles office By mail: Mail to your local election official Online: https://www.sec.state.ma.us/ovr/
Michigan	In person: 30 days before Election Day By mail: Postmarked 30 days before Election Day	In person: City or township clerk's office By mail: Mail to city or township clerk

WHERE TO FIND INFORMATION ON THE CANDIDATES	PRIMARY OR CAUCUS? OPEN OR CLOSED?	MAIL-IN VOTING?
https://www.sos.la.gov/ElectionsAndVoting/GetElectionInformation/SearchForCandidates/Pages/default.aspx	Closed primary However, state/local elections follow a top-two primary system.	Yes, for absentee ballots
https://www.politics1.com/me.htm	Closed primary but parties have the option to allow unaffiliated voters to participate.	Yes, for absentee ballots
https://www.baltimoresun.com/politics/elections/voter-guide/	Closed primary	Yes, for absentee ballots
https://www.headcount.org/issues-and-candidates/	Semiclosed primary	Yes, for absentee ballots
https://www.michigan.gov/sos/0,4670,7–127–1633_8716_8735–,00.html	Partially open primary	Yes, for absentee ballots

STATE	DEADLINE TO REGISTER TO VOTE	WHERE AND HOW TO REGISTER
Minnesota	In person: Election Day By mail: Received 21 days before Election Day Online: 21 days before Election Day	In person: Voter registration office or office of election division By mail: Mail to your county's voter registration office or office of election division Online: https://mnvotes.sos.state.mn.us/VoterRegistration/VoterRegistrationMain.aspx
Mississippi	In person: 30 days before Election Day By mail: Postmarked 30 days before Election Day	In person: County circuit clerk's office By mail: Mail to your county's circuit clerk's office
Missouri	In person: 27 days before Election Day By mail: Postmarked 27 days before Election Day Online: 27 days before Election Day	In person: Local election authority By mail: Mail to your county's voter registration office or office of election division Online: https://s1.sos.mo.gov/votemissouri/request
Montana	By 5 P.M. 30 days before the election Late registering is available through the end of Election Day	In person: County election office By mail: Mail the voter registration form to the county election administrator
Nebraska	In person: 11 days before Election Day Online: 18 days before Election Day	In person: County election office Online: Use the NEReg2Vote portal at https://www.nebraska.gov/apps-sos-voter-registration/

WHERE TO FIND INFORMATION ON THE CANDIDATES	PRIMARY OR CAUCUS? OPEN OR CLOSED?	MAIL-IN VOTING?
https://politics1.com/mn.htm	Partially open primary	Yes, for absentee ballots
https://www.sos.ms.gov/Elections-Voting/Pages/Candidate-Information.aspx	Open primary	Yes, for absentee ballots
https://www.sos.mo.gov/elections/candidates	Open primary	Yes, for absentee ballots
Local newspapers; state political parties' websites; https://www.politics1.com/mt.htm	Open primary	No
http://www.sos.nebraska.gov/elec/candidateinfo.html	Top-two primary system (the two candidates with the most votes, regardless of party, advance to the general election).	Yes, but must meet certain criteria

STATE	DEADLINE TO REGISTER TO VOTE	WHERE AND HOW TO REGISTER
Nevada	In person: 21 days before Election Day Mail: Postmarked 28 days before Election Day Online: 19 days before Election Day	In person: Any department of motor vehicles office, county clerk or registrar of voters' offices, various social services agencies, or college campuses By mail: Mail to local county clerk or registrar of voters' office Online: RegisterToVoteNV.gov
New Hampshire	In person: 6 to 13 days before Election Day, depending on the date set by the local supervisors of the checklist Same-day registration is permitted on Election Day	Local town or city clerk's office
New Jersey	In person: 21 days before Election Day	By mail or deliver the voter registration application to the local county commissioner of registration or superintendent of elections
New Mexico	In person: 28 days before Election Day	Mail the voter registration form to the New Mexico Office of the Secretary of State or the local county clerk's office
New York	In person: 25 days before Election Day	In person: Local county board of elections, agency-based voter registration center, or department of motor vehicles By mail: Local county board of elections

WHERE TO FIND INFORMATION ON THE CANDIDATES	PRIMARY OR CAUCUS? OPEN OR CLOSED?	MAIL-IN VOTING?
Local newspapers; https://www.politics1.com/nv.htm	Closed primary (state elections); caucus (presidential elections).	Yes, if there were not more than 20 votes registered in a precinct in the last general election
https://www.citizenscount.org/elections	Semiclosed primary (must be registered as a party member to vote in that party's primary, but a previously unaffiliated voter may participate in the primary of their choice).	No
Local media; https://www.politics1.com/nj.htm	Semiclosed primary (must be registered as a party member to vote in that party's primary, but a previously unaffiliated voter may participate in the primary of their choice).	Yes, for municipalities with a population of less than 500 people
sos.state.nm.us/candidate-and-campaigns	Closed primary	No
Local newspapers; https://www.politics1.com/ny.htm	Closed primary	No

STATE	DEADLINE TO REGISTER TO VOTE	WHERE AND HOW TO REGISTER
North Carolina	25 days before Election Day Same-day registration is permitted during early voting	In person: NC State Board of Elections, county boards of elections, public libraries, public high schools or college admissions offices, or certain state agencies By mail: Local county board of elections
North Dakota	Does not require voter registration. A person may vote if they provide acceptable identification.	N/A
Ohio	30 days before Election Day	In person: Secretary of state's office, county boards of elections, office of the registrar of the Ohio Bureau of Motor Vehicles, public libraries, public high schools or vocational schools, county treasurers' offices, or offices of certain designated agencies By mail: Secretary of state's office or county board of elections Online: olvr.sos.state.oh.us
Oklahoma	25 days before Election Day	By mail: To state election board However, if the application is obtained from the MVA or a government agency offering public assistance, the relevant agency will mail it to the state elections board upon completion
Oregon	21 days before Election Day	By mail: Local county elections office Online: sos.oregon.gov
Pennsylvania	30 days before Election Day	By mail: Local county voter registration office Online: pavoterservices.pa.gov

WHERE TO FIND INFORMATION ON THE CANDIDATES	PRIMARY OR CAUCUS? OPEN OR CLOSED?	MAIL-IN VOTING?
The NC State Board of Elections Voters' Guide; https://www.politics1.com/nc.htm	Partially closed primary (parties may choose to let in unaffiliated voters, while excluding members of opposing parties).	No
Local newspapers; https://www.politics1.com/nd.htm	Open primary (state elections); firehouse caucus (presidential elections). This is essentially a primary, but with fewer polling places.	Yes
https://www.politics1.com/oh.htm	Partially open primary (voters may cross party lines, but they must publicly declare their ballot choice or their ballot selection is regarded as a registration with the corresponding party).	No
OK Policy Institute, local newspapers; https://www.politics1.com/ok.htm	Partially closed primary (parties may choose to let in unaffiliated voters, while excluding members of opposing parties).	No
Voter pamphlets are mailed to each address in Oregon; https://www.politics1.com/or.htm	Closed primary	Yes
https://www.pavoterservices.pa.gov/ElectionInfo/electioninfo.aspx	Closed primary	No

STATE	DEADLINE TO REGISTER TO VOTE	WHERE AND HOW TO REGISTER
Rhode Island	30 days before Election Day	By mail: Local board of canvassers or RI Board of Elections Online: elections.ri.gov
South Carolina	30 days before Election Day	In person and mail: Local county board of voter registration Online: scvotes.org
South Dakota	15 days before Election Day Postmarked 30 days prior to election	In person: County auditor's office, driver's license station, City Finance office, public assistance agencies, Department of Human Services offices, and military recruitment offices By mail: Local county auditor's office.
Tennessee	30 days before Election Day	In person: During transactions with certain state agencies By mail: Local county election commission Online: ovr.govote.tn.gov
Texas	30 days before Election Day	By mail to local voter registrar's office
Utah	In person or by mail: 30 days before Election Day Online: 7 days before Election Day Same-day registration is permitted through Election Day	In person and by mail: Utah County Clerk, Elections Office 100 East Center Street, Rm 3100 Provo, Utah 84606 Online: vote.utah.gov

WHERE TO FIND INFORMATION ON THE CANDIDATES	PRIMARY OR CAUCUS? OPEN OR CLOSED?	MAIL-IN VOTING?
http://sos.ri.gov/candidates/	Semiclosed primary (must be registered as a party member to vote in that party's primary, but a previously unaffiliated voter may participate in the primary of their choice).	No
https://www.sciway.net/sc-elections/	Open primary	No
https://sdsos.gov/elections-voting/upcoming-elections/general-information/default.aspx	Partially closed primary (parties may choose to let in unaffiliated voters, while excluding members of opposing parties)	No
Local newspapers; https://www.politics1.com/tn.htm	Partially open primary (voters may cross party lines, but they must publicly declare their ballot choice or their ballot selection is regarded as a registration with the corresponding party).	No
https://my.lwv.org/texas/voting-elections/voters-guide	Open primary	No
Voter pamphlets are mailed to every address in the state; https://www.politics1.com/ut.htm	Partially closed primary (parties may choose to let in unaffiliated voters, while excluding members of opposing parties).	Yes

STATE	DEADLINE TO REGISTER TO VOTE	WHERE AND HOW TO REGISTER
Vermont	Same-day registration is permitted through Election Day	In person and by mail: Local town or city clerk's office Online: olvr.sec.state.vt.us
Virginia	22 days before Election Day	By mail: Local registrar's office or Virginia Department of Elections Online: elections.virginia.gov
Washington	In person: 8 days before Election Day By mail or online: 29 days before Election Day Same-day registration is permitted on Election Day	In person and by mail: Local county elections office Online: sos.wa.gov
West Virginia	21 days before Election Day	In person and by mail: Secretary of state's office or local county clerk's office Online: ovr.sos.wv.gov
Wisconsin	20 days before Election Day Same-day registration is permitted on Election Day	In person: Local municipal clerk's office or special registration deputy Online: myvote.wi.gov
Wyoming	14 days before Election Day Same-day registration is permitted on Election Day	In person and by mail: Local county clerk's office

WHERE TO FIND INFORMATION ON THE CANDIDATES	PRIMARY OR CAUCUS? OPEN OR CLOSED?	MAIL-IN VOTING?
Local newspapers; https://www.sec.state.vt.us/elections/candidates.aspx	Open primary	No
https://www.elections.virginia.gov/casting-a-ballot/candidate-list/index.html	Open primary	No
https://www.sos.wa.gov/elections/voters-guide/2020/presidential-primary-voters-guide.aspx	Top-two primary system (the two candidates with the most votes, regardless of party, advance to the general election)	Yes
https://services.sos.wv.gov/apps/elections/candidate-search/	Semiclosed primary (must be registered as a party member to vote in that party's primary, but a previously unaffiliated voter may participate in the primary of their choice)	No
https://www.wisconsinvote.org/candidates-and-races	Open primary	No
Voters may obtain a voter pamphlet from the Office of the WY Secretary of State; https://www.politics1.com/wy.htm	Partially open primary for state elections (voters may cross party lines, but they must publicly declare their ballot choice or their ballot selection is regarded as a registration with the corresponding party); caucus for presidential elections	Yes, but for special elections only

State-by-State Voter Identification Requirements

There are currently fifteen states that do not require any documentation to vote: California, Oregon, Nevada, New Mexico, Wyoming, Nebraska, Minnesota, Illinois, North Carolina, Maryland, Vermont, New Jersey, New York, Maine, and Massachusetts. Each of these states must meet federal HAVA (Help America Vote Act) requirements for first-time voters.

STATE	WHAT TO BRING TO THE POLLS
Alabama	Valid forms of ID include: • Valid Alabama driver's license • Valid Alabama nondriver ID • Valid Alabama photo voter ID card • Valid state-issued ID (Alabama or any other state) • Valid federal-issued ID • Valid US passport • Valid employee ID from federal government • Valid employee ID from Alabama, county, municipality, board, or other entity of this state • Valid student or employee ID from a public or private college or university in the state of Alabama (including postgraduate technical or professional schools) • Valid military ID • Valid tribal ID

STATE	WHAT TO BRING TO THE POLLS
Alaska	Valid forms of ID include: • Voter ID card • Driver's license • State ID • Military ID • Passport • Hunting or fishing license • Other current or valid photo ID
Arizona	Valid forms of photo ID include: • Driver's license • Nonoperating identification card • Tribal enrollment card or other for tribal identification • United States federal, state, or local government-issued identification Valid forms of nonphoto ID include: • Utility bill of the elector that is dated within 90 days of the date of election • Bank or credit union statement that is dated within 90 days of the election • Valid Arizona vehicle registration • Indian census card • Property tax statement of the elector's residence • Tribal enrollment card or other form of tribal identification • Arizona vehicle insurance card • Recorder's certificate • Valid US federal, state, or local government-issued identification, including a voter registration card issued by the county recorder • Any mailing to the elector marked "Official Election Material"

STATE	WHAT TO BRING TO THE POLLS
Arkansas	Valid forms of ID must show the name and address of the voter, including a current and valid photo ID, or a current utility bill, bank statement, government check, paycheck, or other government document
Colorado	Valid forms of ID include: • Valid Colorado driver's license or valid identification card issued by the Colorado Department of Revenue • Valid US passport • Valid employee identification card with a photograph of the eligible elector issued by any branch, department, agency, or entity of the US government or of Colorado, or by any county, municipality, board, authority, or other political subdivision of Colorado • Valid pilot's license issued by the Federal Aviation Administration or other authorized agency of the US • Valid US military identification card with a photograph of the eligible elector • Copy of a current (within the last 60 days) utility bill, bank statement, government check, paycheck, or other government document that shows the name and address of the elector • Certificate of degree of Indian or Alaskan Native blood • Valid Medicare or Medicaid card issued by the Centers for Medicare and Medicaid Services • Certified copy of a US birth certificate for the elector • Certified documentation of naturalization • Valid student identification card with a photograph of the eligible elector issued by an institute of higher education in Colorado • Valid veteran identification card issued by the US Department of Veterans Affairs with a photograph of the eligible elector • Valid identification card issued by a federally recognized tribal government certifying tribal membership

STATE	WHAT TO BRING TO THE POLLS
Colorado (cont.)	• Any form of identification listed above that shows your address; must show a Colorado address to qualify as an acceptable form of identification
Connecticut	First-time voters must present a copy of a current and valid photo identification that shows your name and address; or a copy of a current utility bill, bank statement, government check, paycheck, or government document that shows your name and address; or cast a provisional ballot. Other voters must present Social Security card, or any preprinted form of identification that shows your name and address, or name and signature, or name and photograph, or sign a statement under penalty of false statement on Form ED-681 entitled, "Signatures of Electors Who Did Not Present ID."
Delaware	Nonphoto ID is requested. If you do not have an approved form of ID, an affidavit is available. Valid forms of ID include: • Valid Delaware driver's license or ID card • Current utility bill, bank statement, or government pay stub
Florida	Valid forms of ID include: • Valid Florida driver's license • Florida identification card issued by the DMV • US passport • Debit or credit card • Military identification • Student identification • Retirement center identification • Neighborhood association identification • Public assistance identification

STATE	WHAT TO BRING TO THE POLLS
Florida (cont.)	• Veteran health identification card issued by the United States Department of Veterans Affairs • License to carry a concealed weapon or firearm • Employee identification card issued by any branch, department, agency, or entity of the federal government, the state, a county, or a municipality
Georgia	Photo ID is required to vote in Georgia. Valid forms of photo ID include: • Georgia driver's license, even if expired • Any valid state or federal government-issued photo ID, including a free ID card issued by your county registrar's office or the Georgia Department of Driver Services (DDS) • Valid employee photo ID from any branch, department, agency, or entity of the US government, Georgia, or any county, municipality, board, authority, or other entity of this state • US passport ID • US military photo ID • Valid tribal photo ID
Hawaii	Valid forms of ID include: • Valid Hawaii driver's license or ID card • Current utility bill • Current bank statement • Current government or other paycheck • Any other government document that shows your name and address
Idaho	Photo ID is required to vote in Idaho. Valid forms of ID include: • Valid Idaho driver's license or photo identification card • US passport or federal photo identification card • Tribal photo identification card

STATE	WHAT TO BRING TO THE POLLS
Idaho (cont)	• Current student photo ID issued by an Idaho high school or postsecondary education institution • License to carry a concealed weapon issued by a county sheriff in Idaho
Indiana	Photo ID is required to vote in Indiana. Valid forms of ID include: • Valid Indiana driver's license • Indiana photo ID card • Military ID or US passport
Iowa	Photo ID is requested to vote at the polls in Iowa. Valid forms of ID include: • Iowa driver's license • Iowa nonoperator's ID • US passport • Military ID • Veteran's ID • Voter ID card
Kansas	Photo ID is required to vote in Kansas. Valid forms of ID include: • Driver's license or nondriver's identification card issued by Kansas or by another state or district of the United States • Concealed carry of handgun license issued by Kansas or a concealed carry of handgun or weapon license issued by another state or district of the United States • US passport • Employee badge or identification document issued by a municipal, county, state, or federal government office • Military identification document issued by the United States

STATE	WHAT TO BRING TO THE POLLS
Kansas (cont.)	• Student identification card issued by an accredited postsecondary institution of education in the state of Kansas • Public assistance identification card issued by a municipal, county, state, or federal government office • Identification card issued by an Indian tribe
Kentucky	Valid forms of ID include: • Driver's license • Social Security card, or credit card, or other photo IDs that have picture and signature of voter
Louisiana	Photo ID is required to vote in Louisiana. Valid forms of ID include: • Valid Louisiana driver's license • Louisiana special identification card or other generally recognized picture identification card that contains the name and signature of the applicant
Michigan	Photo ID is requested to vote in Michigan. Valid forms of ID include: • Valid employee ID from federal government • Federal or state government-issued photo ID • US passport • Military identification card with photo • Student identification with photo from a high school or an accredited institution of higher education • Tribal identification card with photo

STATE	WHAT TO BRING TO THE POLLS
Mississippi	Photo ID is required to vote in Mississippi. Valid forms of ID include: • A driver's license/photo ID card issued by a branch, department, or entity of the state of Mississippi • US passport • Government employee ID card • Firearms license • Student photo ID issued by an accredited Mississippi university, college, or community/junior college • US military ID • Tribal photo ID • Any other photo ID issued by any branch, department, agency or entity of the United States government or any state government • Mississippi voter identification card
Missouri	Photo ID is required to vote in Missouri. Valid forms of photo ID include: • Missouri driver's license • Missouri nondriver's license • US passport • US military ID If you do not have a photo ID, you may show one of the following along with a signed statement: • Voter registration card • ID from a Missouri university, college, vocational, or technical school • Utility bill • Bank statement • Government check • Paycheck • Other government document showing your name and address

STATE	WHAT TO BRING TO THE POLLS
Montana	Valid forms of ID include: • Driver's license • Photo ID showing your name • Current utility bill, bank statement, paycheck, voter registration confirmation, government check, or other government document showing the elector's current name and current address
New Hampshire	Photo ID is requested to vote in New Hampshire. Valid forms of ID include: • Driver's license issued by any state or federal government • Nondriver ID card issued by NH DMV or motor vehicle agency of another state • Photo ID card for "voting identification only" issued by NH DMV (RSA 260:21) • US armed services identification card • US passport or passcard • NH student ID card • Photo ID not mentioned above, but determined to be legitimate by the moderator, supervisors of the checklist, or clerk of a town, ward, or city. If any person authorized to challenge a voter does so under this provision, the voter shall be required to fill out a challenged voter affidavit before obtaining a ballot. An acceptable photo ID must have an expiration date or date of issuance.

STATE	WHAT TO BRING TO THE POLLS
North Dakota	Photo ID is required to vote in North Dakota. Valid forms of ID include: • Current ND driver's license or nondriver's identification card • Tribal government-issued identification • Long-term care certificate provided by an ND facility
Ohio	Valid forms of ID include: • Unexpired Ohio driver's license or state identification card with present or former address so long as the voter's present residential address is printed in the official list of registered voters for that precinct • Military identification • Photo identification that was issued by the United States government or the state of Ohio that contains the voter's name and current address and that has an expiration date that has not passed • Original or copy of a current utility bill with the voter's name and present address • Original or copy of a current bank statement with the voter's name and present address • Original or copy of a current government check with the voter's name and present address • Original or copy of a current paycheck with the voter's name and present address • Original or copy of a current other government document (other than a notice of voter registration mailed by a board of elections) that shows the voter's name and present address

STATE	WHAT TO BRING TO THE POLLS
Oklahoma	State- or federal-issued photo ID, or an official Oklahoma voter registration card, containing the following information is required to vote in Oklahoma: • Name of the person to whom it was issued • Photograph of the person to whom it was issued • Expiration date that is after the date of the election, unless the identification is valid indefinitely The law requires the voter's name on the proof of identity document to "substantially conform" to the voter's name in the precinct registry. In other words, your name on your proof of identity must match your name in the precinct registry. https://www.ok.gov/elections/Voter_Info/Proof_of_Identity/index.html.
Pennsylvania	No photo ID is required except for first-time voters who must bring photo ID. Valid forms of ID include: • PA driver's license or PennDOT ID card, or ID issued by any PA Commonwealth agency • ID issued by the US government • US passport • US armed forces ID • Student ID • Employee ID If you do not have one of the above types of photo ID, you may use: • Confirmation issued by the county voter registration office • Nonphoto ID issued by any PA commonwealth • Nonphoto ID issued by the US government • Firearm permit • Current utility bill • Current bank statement • Current paycheck • Government check

STATE	WHAT TO BRING TO THE POLLS
Rhode Island	Photo ID is required to vote in Rhode Island. Valid forms of photo ID include: • RI driver's license/permit • US passport • ID card issued by any federally recognized tribal government • ID card issued by an educational institution in the United States • US military identification card • ID card issued by the US government or state of Rhode Island (RIPTA bus pass, etc.) • Government-issued medical card • RI Voter ID card
South Carolina	Photo ID is required to vote in South Carolina. Valid forms of ID include: • South Carolina driver's license • South Carolina DMV ID card • South Carolina voter registration card with photo • Federal military ID • US passport • Concealed weapons permit

STATE	WHAT TO BRING TO THE POLLS
South Dakota	Photo ID is required to vote in South Dakota. Valid forms of ID include: • South Dakota driver's license or nondriver ID card • US government photo ID (passport is acceptable) • US armed forces ID • Current student photo identification card from a South Dakota high school or South Dakota accredited institution of higher education • Tribal photo ID
Tennessee	Photo ID is required to vote in Tennessee. Valid forms of ID include: • Tennessee driver's license with your photo • US passport • Photo ID issued by the Tennessee Department of Safety and Homeland Security • Photo ID issued by the federal or Tennessee state government • US military photo ID • Tennessee handgun carry permit with your photo
Texas	Photo ID is required to vote in Texas. Valid forms of ID include: • Texas driver's license issued by the Texas Department of Public Safety (DPS) • Texas election identification certificate issued by DPS • Texas personal identification card issued by DPS • Texas license to carry a handgun issued by DPS • US military identification card containing the person's photograph • US citizenship certificate containing the person's photograph • US passport

STATE	WHAT TO BRING TO THE POLLS
Utah	One photo ID, or two nonphoto IDs, is/are required to vote in Utah. Valid forms of ID include: • Currently valid Utah driver's license • Currently valid ID card issued by the state or a branch, department, or agency of the United States • Valid Utah permit to carry a concealed weapon • Currently valid US passport or valid tribal ID card, whether or not the card includes a photograph of the voter If voters don't have one of the above IDs, they can instead bring two of the following: • Current utility bill or copy thereof dated within 90 days before the election • Bank or other financial account statement or legible copy • Certified birth certificate • Valid Social Security card • Check issued by the state or federal government or legible copy thereof • Paycheck from the voter's employer, or legible copy • Currently valid Utah hunting or fishing license • Currently valid US military ID card • Certified naturalization documents (NOT a green card) • Certified copy of court records showing the voter's adoption or name change • Bureau of Indian Affairs card or tribal treaty card • Valid Medicaid or Medicare or Electronic Benefits Transfer card • Currently valid ID card issued by a local government within the state • Valid ID card issued by an employer • Valid ID card issued by a college, university, technical school, or professional school within the state • Current Utah vehicle registration

STATE	WHAT TO BRING TO THE POLLS
Virginia	Photo ID is required to vote in Virginia. Valid forms of ID include: • Valid Virginia driver's license or identification card • Valid Virginia DMV-issued veteran's ID card • Valid US passport • Other government-issued photo identification cards (must be issued by US government, the commonwealth of Virginia, or a political subdivision of the commonwealth) • Tribal enrollment or other tribal ID issued by one of eleven tribes recognized by the commonwealth of Virginia • Valid college or university student photo identification card (must be from an institution of higher education located in Virginia) • Valid student ID issued by a public school or private school in Virginia displaying a photo • Employee identification card containing a photograph of the voter and issued by an employer of the voter in the ordinary course of the employer's business
Washington	Photo ID is not required if voting in person in Washington, but voters must sign a declaration.

STATE	WHAT TO BRING TO THE POLLS
West Virginia	Voter ID is required to vote in West Virginia in person on Election Day or during the early voting period. Acceptable forms of nonphoto identification include: • Voter registration card • Medicare card or Social Security card • Birth certificate • WV hunting or fishing license • WV SNAP ID card • WV TANF program ID card • WV Medicaid ID card • Bank or debit card • Utility bill or bank statement issued within six months of the date of the election • Health insurance card issued to the voter Acceptable forms of photo identification include: • WV driver's license or other WV ID card issued by the DMV • Driver's license issued by another state • US passport or passport card • Military ID card issued by the US • US or WV government employee ID card • Student ID card • A concealed carry (pistol/revolver) permit

STATE	WHAT TO BRING TO THE POLLS
Wisconsin	Photo ID is required to vote in Wisconsin. Valid forms of ID include: • Wisconsin DOT-issued driver's license, even if driving privileges are revoked or suspended • Wisconsin DOT-issued identification card • Military ID card issued by the US uniformed services (including retired and dependent uniformed service IDs) • US passport book or card • Certificate of naturalization (that was issued no earlier than two years before the date of the election) • Identification card issued by a federally recognized Indian tribe in Wisconsin (can be expired or unexpired) • Driver's license receipt issued by Wisconsin DOT (valid for 45 days from date issued) • Identification card receipt issued by Wisconsin DOT (valid for 45 days from date issued) • Wisconsin DMV ID petition process photo receipt (valid for 180 days from date issued) • Veteran Affairs ID card (must be unexpired or have no expiration date) • A photo identification card issued by a Wisconsin accredited university or college, or technical college that contains the following: date the card was issued, signature of student, expiration date no later than two years after date of issuance. The university or college ID must be accompanied by a separate document that proves enrollment, such as a tuition fee receipt, enrollment verification letter, or class schedule. Enrollment verification document can be shown electronically.

Same-Day Registration

Most states do not offer the opportunity to register to vote on the same day as elections. The following states allow same-day voter registration with specific requirements and documentation.

STATE	SAME-DAY REGISTRATION
California	If you did not register to vote by the 15-day voter registration deadline, in most elections, you may conditionally register to vote and cast a provisional ballot by visiting your county elections office during the period of 14 days prior to, and including, Election Day. Once your county elections official processes your affidavit of registration, determines your eligibility to register, and validates your information, your registration becomes permanent and your provisional ballot will be counted.
Colorado	If you miss the registration deadline to receive a ballot in the mail, you can register in person at a voter service and polling center through Election Day.
Connecticut	Connecticut offers the opportunity to register to vote on Election Day. Election Day registration is not available at polling places and is only available at one designated location in each town. Election Day registration begins at 6 A.M. and ends at 8 P.M. To vote on Election Day, voters must provide proof of identity and residency.
District of Columbia	The District of Columbia offers the opportunity to register to vote on Election Day only. Voters may do so at the assigned polling place or at any early voting center. To register, voters must provide proof of residency.
Hawaii	In Hawaii, you can register to vote at your county's early walk-in voting locations during the early voting period or at your assigned polling place on Election Day.

Idaho	Idaho offers the opportunity to register to vote on Election Day at the polls. To register on Election Day, voters need proof of ID and proof of residence.
Illinois	Illinois offers the opportunity to register to vote on Election Day at your home precinct. To register, voters must bring two pieces of identification: one must have their current address, and the other should be another form of ID.
Iowa	Iowa offers the opportunity to register to vote on Election Day. To register on Election Day, voters must go to the polling place for their current address and show proof of identity and residency. If you cannot prove who you are or where you live, another voter from your precinct may attest for you.
Maryland	Maryland offers the opportunity to register to vote during the early voting period only at your polling place. To register, voters must have an MD driver's license/state ID and proof of residency.
Michigan	Michigan offers the opportunity to register to vote if voters did not register by 15 days before the election. Voters may register after the deadline, and including on Election Day, by bringing the voter registration form and residency verification to the local city/township clerk.
Minnesota	Minnesota offers the opportunity to register to vote on Election Day. Voters must bring proof of residence to register or, if you do not have that information, another registered voter from your precinct may attest to your address.
Montana	Montana offers the opportunity to register to vote on Election Day at your county election office before 8:00 P.M. https://app.mt.gov/voterinfo/
New Hampshire	New Hampshire offers the opportunity to register to vote on Election Day at the polling place. You will be asked to show proof of age, citizenship, and domicile.

North Carolina	North Carolina offers the opportunity to register to vote during the early voting period only, between 6:30 A.M. and 7:30 P.M. at your home polling place. Voters must show a piece of ID with name and current address.
Rhode Island	In presidential elections only, unregistered and eligible citizens can register and vote for president and vice president at their local board of canvassers.
Vermont	Vermont offers the opportunity to register to vote on any day up to and including Election Day at your city clerk's office during their normal business hours.
Wisconsin	Wisconsin offers the opportunity to register to vote on Election Day during polling hours at your precinct. To register on Election Day, voters must show an approved form of ID and proof of residence.
Wyoming	Wyoming offers voters the opportunity to register to vote on Election Day at the precinct in which they are a resident, and voters must provide either a valid WY driver's license or the last four digits of their SSN.

State-by-State Voting Rights of Felons

STATE	CAN FELONS VOTE WHILE INCARCERATED?	WHILE ON PAROLE FOR A FELONY?	CAN VOTING RIGHTS BE RESTORED?	ARE THERE ANY CRIMES WHERE RIGHTS CANNOT BE RESTORED?	ARE VOTING RIGHTS RESTORED AUTOMATICALLY?	WHAT PROCESS IS REQUIRED TO RESTORE VOTING RIGHTS?	DO YOU HAVE TO REREGISTER?
Alabama	No	No	Yes	Treason, impeachment, rape, murder, incest, and sexual crimes against children	No	Apply for a Certificate of Eligibility to Register to Vote from the Board of Pardons and Paroles	Yes
Alaska	No	Depends on crime	Yes	Certain violent felons are ineligible to vote in prison, parole, and probation	Yes		Yes

STATE	CAN FELONS VOTE WHILE INCARCERATED?	WHILE ON PAROLE FOR A FELONY?	CAN VOTING RIGHTS BE RESTORED?	ARE THERE ANY CRIMES WHERE RIGHTS CANNOT BE RESTORED?	ARE VOTING RIGHTS RESTORED AUTOMATICALLY?	WHAT PROCESS IS REQUIRED TO RESTORE VOTING RIGHTS?	DO YOU HAVE TO REREGISTER?
Arizona	No	No	Yes	People who were sentenced to lifetime probation	Yes—for first-time felony conviction only (single offense, not single case that may have multiple offenses)	Petition the court that sentenced you to have rights restored. If imprisoned, must wait 2 years after completed prison sentence and any period of parole/community supervision	Yes
Arkansas	No	No	Yes		No	Must provide county clerk proof that you have satisfied all terms of sentence and paid all fines, costs, and restitution	Yes

STATE	CAN FELONS VOTE WHILE INCARCERATED?	WHILE ON PAROLE FOR A FELONY?	CAN VOTING RIGHTS BE RESTORED?	ARE THERE ANY CRIMES WHERE RIGHTS CANNOT BE RESTORED?	ARE VOTING RIGHTS RESTORED AUTOMATICALLY?	WHAT PROCESS IS REQUIRED TO RESTORE VOTING RIGHTS?	DO YOU HAVE TO REREGISTER?
California	No	No	Yes		Yes		Yes
Colorado	No	Yes	Yes		Yes		Yes
Connecticut	No	No	Yes		Yes, upon completion of parole and payment of fines		Yes
Delaware	No	No	Yes	Murder or manslaughter, (except vehicular homicide); an offense against public administration involving bribery or improper influence or abuse of office, or any like offense; or a sexual offense	Yes	Finishing all terms of service or pardon except for the crimes listed	

STATE	CAN FELONS VOTE WHILE INCARCERATED?	WHILE ON PAROLE FOR A FELONY?	CAN VOTING RIGHTS BE RESTORED?	ARE THERE ANY CRIMES WHERE RIGHTS CANNOT BE RESTORED?	ARE VOTING RIGHTS RESTORED AUTOMATICALLY?	WHAT PROCESS IS REQUIRED TO RESTORE VOTING RIGHTS?	DO YOU HAVE TO REREGISTER?
Florida	No	No	Yes		Yes, except murder or sexual felonies	For murder or sexual felonies you can apply for a restoration of civil rights	Yes
Georgia	No	No	Yes		Yes	Completion of supervised release	Yes
Hawaii	No	Yes	Yes		Yes		Yes

STATE	CAN FELONS VOTE WHILE INCARCERATED?	WHILE ON PAROLE FOR A FELONY?	CAN VOTING RIGHTS BE RESTORED?	ARE THERE ANY CRIMES WHERE RIGHTS CANNOT BE RESTORED?	ARE VOTING RIGHTS RESTORED AUTOMATICALLY?	WHAT PROCESS IS REQUIRED TO RESTORE VOTING RIGHTS?	DO YOU HAVE TO REREGISTER?
Idaho	No	No	Yes	• Murder • Voluntary manslaughter • Rape • Kidnapping • Lewd conduct w/a minor child • Manufacture of a controlled substance • Delivery of a controlled substance • Intent to manufacture a controlled substance • Intent to deliver a controlled substance	Yes		
Illinois	No	Yes	Yes		Yes		
Indiana	No	Yes	Yes		Yes		Yes

STATE	CAN FELONS VOTE WHILE INCARCERATED?	WHILE ON PAROLE FOR A FELONY?	CAN VOTING RIGHTS BE RESTORED?	ARE THERE ANY CRIMES WHERE RIGHTS CANNOT BE RESTORED?	ARE VOTING RIGHTS RESTORED AUTOMATICALLY?	WHAT PROCESS IS REQUIRED TO RESTORE VOTING RIGHTS?	DO YOU HAVE TO REREGISTER?
Iowa	No	No	Yes		No	Apply for a Restoration of Voting Rights and pay off all outstanding debts	
Kansas	No	No	Yes		Yes		Yes
Kentucky	No	No	Yes		No	Governor must grant restoration of civil rights; contact local parole officer to apply	
Louisiana	No	No	Yes		Yes, as of March 1, 2019	Must provide proof of completion of your sentence to local registrar	Yes

STATE	CAN FELONS VOTE WHILE INCARCERATED?	WHILE ON PAROLE FOR A FELONY?	CAN VOTING RIGHTS BE RESTORED?	ARE THERE ANY CRIMES WHERE RIGHTS CANNOT BE RESTORED?	ARE VOTING RIGHTS RESTORED AUTOMATICALLY?	WHAT PROCESS IS REQUIRED TO RESTORE VOTING RIGHTS?	DO YOU HAVE TO REREGISTER?
Maine	Yes	Yes	N/A				
Maryland	No	Yes	Yes	Buying and selling votes	Yes		Yes
Massachusetts	No	Yes	Yes		Yes		Yes
Michigan	No	Yes	Yes		Yes		Yes
Minnesota	No	No	Yes		Yes		Yes

STATE	CAN FELONS VOTE WHILE INCARCERATED?	WHILE ON PAROLE FOR A FELONY?	CAN VOTING RIGHTS BE RESTORED?	ARE THERE ANY CRIMES WHERE RIGHTS CANNOT BE RESTORED?	ARE VOTING RIGHTS RESTORED AUTOMATICALLY?	WHAT PROCESS IS REQUIRED TO RESTORE VOTING RIGHTS?	DO YOU HAVE TO REREGISTER?
Mississippi	No	No	Yes	Treason or impeachment or one or more of 22 crimes such as arson, armed robbery, bigamy, theft, statutory rape, murder		Clemency granted by the governor; may also petition their state representative in the legislature to pass a bill allowing them to vote; however, may still vote for the president in federal elections	
Missouri	No	No	Yes	Convicted of an election offense	Yes		
Montana	No	Yes	Yes				Yes

STATE	CAN FELONS VOTE WHILE INCARCERATED?	WHILE ON PAROLE FOR A FELONY?	CAN VOTING RIGHTS BE RESTORED?	ARE THERE ANY CRIMES WHERE RIGHTS CANNOT BE RESTORED?	ARE VOTING RIGHTS RESTORED AUTOMATICALLY?	WHAT PROCESS IS REQUIRED TO RESTORE VOTING RIGHTS?	DO YOU HAVE TO REREGISTER?
Nebraska	No	No	Yes	Treason—not automatically restored; must apply for restoration of civil rights	Yes, 2 full years after completion of all of your sentence including probation and parole		Yes
Nevada	No	Yes	Yes		Yes		Yes
New Hampshire	No	Yes	Yes		Yes		Yes
New Jersey	No	No	Yes		Yes		Yes

STATE	CAN FELONS VOTE WHILE INCARCERATED?	WHILE ON PAROLE FOR A FELONY?	CAN VOTING RIGHTS BE RESTORED?	ARE THERE ANY CRIMES WHERE RIGHTS CANNOT BE RESTORED?	ARE VOTING RIGHTS RESTORED AUTOMATICALLY?	WHAT PROCESS IS REQUIRED TO RESTORE VOTING RIGHTS?	DO YOU HAVE TO REREGISTER?
New Mexico	No	No	Yes		Yes		Yes
New York	No	No	Yes		Yes	Finishing incarceration and parole OR a pardon	
North Carolina	No	No	Yes		Yes		Yes
North Dakota	No	Yes	Yes		Yes		Yes

STATE	CAN FELONS VOTE WHILE INCARCERATED?	WHILE ON PAROLE FOR A FELONY?	CAN VOTING RIGHTS BE RESTORED?	ARE THERE ANY CRIMES WHERE RIGHTS CANNOT BE RESTORED?	ARE VOTING RIGHTS RESTORED AUTOMATICALLY?	WHAT PROCESS IS REQUIRED TO RESTORE VOTING RIGHTS?	DO YOU HAVE TO REREGISTER?
Ohio	No	Yes	Yes	Twice convicted of an election crime causes a permanent bar from voting in Ohio	Yes		Yes
Oklahoma	No		Yes			Pardon or after time equal to original sentence; may not vote from the time of judgment and sentencing until the full sentence has expired, regardless if you are paroled	Yes
Oregon	No	Yes	Yes		Yes		Yes

STATE	CAN FELONS VOTE WHILE INCARCERATED?	WHILE ON PAROLE FOR A FELONY?	CAN VOTING RIGHTS BE RESTORED?	ARE THERE ANY CRIMES WHERE RIGHTS CANNOT BE RESTORED?	ARE VOTING RIGHTS RESTORED AUTOMATICALLY ?	WHAT PROCESS IS REQUIRED TO RESTORE VOTING RIGHTS?	DO YOU HAVE TO REREGISTER?
Pennsylvania	No	Yes	Yes	You cannot vote if you violated the Pennsylvania Election Code within the last four years	Yes		
Rhode Island	No	Yes	Yes		Yes		Yes
South Carolina	No	No	Yes		Yes		Yes
South Dakota	No	No	Yes		Yes		Yes

STATE	CAN FELONS VOTE WHILE INCARCERATED?	WHILE ON PAROLE FOR A FELONY?	CAN VOTING RIGHTS BE RESTORED?	ARE THERE ANY CRIMES WHERE RIGHTS CANNOT BE RESTORED?	ARE VOTING RIGHTS RESTORED AUTOMATICALLY?	WHAT PROCESS IS REQUIRED TO RESTORE VOTING RIGHTS?	DO YOU HAVE TO REREGISTER?
Tennessee	No	No	Yes	After May 18, 1981: • Voter fraud • Treason • First-degree murder • Aggravated rape After July 1, 2006: • Voter fraud • Treason • Any degree of murder or rape • Certain felonies involving bribery, misconduct involving public officials and employees, or interference with government operations		Restoration of voting rights form must be completed for each conviction with a different case number. Form must be filled out by an agent (parole/probation officer, or criminal court clerk). Generally, felons convicted of murder, rape, treason, or voter fraud since 1981 must apply to the Board of Probation and Parole to have their voting rights restored.	Yes

STATE	CAN FELONS VOTE WHILE INCARCERATED?	WHILE ON PAROLE FOR A FELONY?	CAN VOTING RIGHTS BE RESTORED?	ARE THERE ANY CRIMES WHERE RIGHTS CANNOT BE RESTORED?	ARE VOTING RIGHTS RESTORED AUTOMATICALLY?	WHAT PROCESS IS REQUIRED TO RESTORE VOTING RIGHTS?	DO YOU HAVE TO REREGISTER?
Texas	No	No	Yes		Yes	Completion of sentence or been pardoned	Yes
Utah	No	Yes	Yes		Yes		Yes
Vermont	Yes	Yes					

STATE	CAN FELONS VOTE WHILE INCARCERATED?	WHILE ON PAROLE FOR A FELONY?	CAN VOTING RIGHTS BE RESTORED?	ARE THERE ANY CRIMES WHERE RIGHTS CANNOT BE RESTORED?	ARE VOTING RIGHTS RESTORED AUTOMATICALLY?	WHAT PROCESS IS REQUIRED TO RESTORE VOTING RIGHTS?	DO YOU HAVE TO REREGISTER?
Virginia	No	No	Yes		No	Contact the secretary of the commonwealth to have voting rights restored by the governor. Violent felons, crimes against minors, and electoral offenses: must wait 3 years before contacting.	Non-violent felons will have votes automatically reinstated but have to fill out an online form
Washington	No	No	Yes		Yes		Yes
West Virginia	No	No	Yes		Yes		Yes

STATE	CAN FELONS VOTE WHILE INCARCERATED?	WHILE ON PAROLE FOR A FELONY?	CAN VOTING RIGHTS BE RESTORED?	ARE THERE ANY CRIMES WHERE RIGHTS CANNOT BE RESTORED?	ARE VOTING RIGHTS RESTORED AUTOMATICALLY?	WHAT PROCESS IS REQUIRED TO RESTORE VOTING RIGHTS?	DO YOU HAVE TO REREGISTER?
Wisconsin	No	No	Yes		Yes		Yes
Wyoming	No		Yes		Depends	First-time nonviolent felons, if they completed their supervision or were discharged from an institution on or after January 1, 2010, will have rights automatically restored. If not, then submit Application for Restoration of Wyoming Voting Right.	Yes

How to Get on the Presidential Ballot

STATE	STATE STATUTE	FEES	SIGNATURES FOR PARTY CANDIDATES
Alabama	Ala. Code tit. 17	$3,480.00 or 2% of base salary for primary party candidates; none for independent candidates.	No signatures for major party candidates
Alaska	Alaska Stat. Ann. § 15.25	$100.00 flat fee	None
Arizona	Ariz. Rev. Stat. Ann. tit. 16, Ch. 3	None	US representative: At least 0.5% of the total number of qualified signers in the district the candidate seeks to represent, but no more than 10%. US senator: 0.25% of the total number of qualified signers but no more than 10%.
Arkansas	Ark. Code Ann. § 7	Fixed by party. For a Democrat senator the fee is $12,000; $20,000 to run as a Republican senator. For the House, it is $15,000 for the Republicans and $10,000 for Democrats. No fee for independents.	No signatures for major party candidates.

SIGNATURE REQUIREMENTS FOR INDEPENDENT CANDIDATES	WHERE TO SUBMIT SIGNATURES/ FORMS	NOTES
Only requires signatures for independent candidates—formulated as 3% of qualified electors who voted for governor in the last general election.	An independent candidate must file a petition with the Alabama secretary of state.	Both the process to establish a new political party and the process to become an independent candidate require petitions.
1% of votes cast in the last general election if independent (2,850).	File with the Alaska Division of Elections at/or before 5:00 P.M. on the day of the primary election.	A declaration also must be made under oath before an authorized officer and must be filed with the Alaska Division of Elections.
3% of all registered voters who are not affiliated with a recognized political party in the district the candidate seeks to represent.	With the Arizona secretary of state.	A candidate may not run as an independent if he or she is representing a party that failed to qualify for the primary election.
3% of votes cast for governor in the last election in the district, not to exceed 2,000 (10,000 for Senate).	An independent candidate must file a political practices pledge, affidavit of eligibility, and notice of candidacy with the Arkansas secretary of state by March 1 in the year of the election.	To establish a political party, a petition containing 10,000 signatures is required, and these signatures must be gathered within a specified 90-day window.

STATE	STATE STATUTE	FEES	SIGNATURES FOR PARTY CANDIDATES
California	Cal. Elec. Code § D. 8 (notably §§ 8020–8028 and §§ 8100–8107)	Filing fee for the House is 1% of the first year's salary for that office. Filing fee to run as a senator is 2% of the first year's salary for that office.	United States representative must file 2,000 signatures. If the number of registered voters in the district in which the candidate seeks nomination is fewer than 2,000, a candidate may submit a petition containing four signatures for each dollar of the filing fee, or 20% of the total number of registered voters in the district in which he or she seeks nomination, whichever is less.
Colorado	Colo. Rev. Stat. Ann. T. 1, art. 4	None	House: 1,500 or 10% of votes cast in last primary (whichever is less). Senate: 10,500, or 1,500 per congressional district. May also be nominated "by assembly" of the major party's delegates.

SIGNATURE REQUIREMENTS FOR INDEPENDENT CANDIDATES	WHERE TO SUBMIT SIGNATURES/ FORMS	NOTES
Same as for party	Nomination papers go to the California secretary of state. The nomination papers must also have 65–100 signatures for candidates seeking the office of United States senator, or 40–60 for candidates seeking to be a United States representative.	All candidates must file a candidate intention statement with the California secretary of state and his or her home county government. Nomination forms include a statement of economic interests, a declaration of candidacy, and nomination papers.
House: 1,500, or 2.5% of votes cast for office in the last election. Senate: 1,000 signatures from each congressional district.	Colorado secretary of state	A candidate must publicly announce his or her intention to run for office. Each candidate must submit an audio recording of the pronunciation of his or her name. If nominated by an assembly, the candidate must submit the audio recording within 10 days of the close of the convention.

STATE	STATE STATUTE	FEES	SIGNATURES FOR PARTY CANDIDATES
Connecticut	Conn. Gen. Stat. Ann. tit. 9, Ch. 153	None	Convention: A candidate must receive at least 15% of the votes cast by convention delegates for the office being sought. Or petition: Signatures of 2% of the total number of members enrolled in that major party in the state.
Delaware	Del. Code Ann. tit. 15, §§ 3001–3405	Filing fees are determined by the major parties for their candidates.	Filing a notice of candidacy: Statewide office (senator)—file with chair of the state committee of his or her party. District office (representative)—file with chair of the county committee of the party. Nomination: Only if no other same-party candidates have filed for candidacy may they be nominated.

SIGNATURE REQUIREMENTS FOR INDEPENDENT CANDIDATES	WHERE TO SUBMIT SIGNATURES/ FORMS	NOTES
Minor party: Sends an "Application for Reservation of Party Designation and Formation of Party Designation Committee" to the Connecticut secretary of state and signatures of 25 registered voters. Also must appoint 2 people who will file a statement that the minor party candidate may run under that party. Independent: Requires a petition with signatures of voters equal to 1% of the votes cast at the most recent election for the office being sought, or 7,500 signatures, whichever is less.	Connecticut secretary of state	Petitions may be sent out as circulations to voters. There are additional requirements for who may be a circulator and get signatures.
Minor party candidates are selected by conventions. Independent: Unaffiliated candidates must collect signatures equal to 1% of all eligible voters as of December 31 of the year prior to the election. They have between July 1 and July 15 to obtain the signatures through circulation.	Notice of candidacy goes to the state election commissioner along with the filing fee.	Petitions are only used by unaffiliated candidates to gain access to the general election ballot and by political party candidates to waive political party filing fees.

STATE	STATE STATUTE	FEES	SIGNATURES FOR PARTY CANDIDATES
Florida	FL ST T. IX, Ch. 99	Partisan: $10,440 (or 6% of annual salary) Independent: $6,960 (or 4% of annual salary)	1% of registered voters in the district
Georgia	Ga. Code Ann. § 21–2	3% of the total gross salary of the office paid in the preceding calendar. Payment and breakdown of the fee is under Ga. Code Ann. § 21–2–131 (West).	Nominated at his or her party's primary election. 0.25% of the total number of registered voters eligible to vote in the last general election if the candidate is seeking statewide office, if they cannot afford the filing fee. 1% of the total number of registered voters eligible to vote in the last election for the office being sought by the candidate if the candidate is seeking an office other than statewide office
Hawaii	Haw. Rev. Stat. Ann. § 12	$75	25 signatures on nomination papers

SIGNATURE REQUIREMENTS FOR INDEPENDENT CANDIDATES	WHERE TO SUBMIT SIGNATURES/ FORMS	NOTES
1% of registered voters in the district	Florida Department of State, Division of Elections	Major party, minor party, and unaffiliated candidates in Florida all file in the same way. Petitions may be used by candidates to waive filing fees. Each signature costs $0.10 to verify.
0.25% of the total number of registered voters eligible to vote in the last general election if the candidate is seeking statewide office. 1% of the total number of registered voters eligible to vote in the last election for the office being sought by the candidate if the candidate is seeking an office other than statewide office.	Georgia secretary of state	In lieu of a filing fee, a candidate may submit a pauper's affidavit and qualifying petition, which certifies that the candidate is unable to pay the fee. Declarations of Candidacy are also required and go to the Georgia secretary of state.
25 signatures on nomination papers	Hawaii Office of Elections	All candidates, regardless of partisan affiliation, must be nominated via the state's primary election before appearing on a general election ballot.

STATE	STATE STATUTE	FEES	SIGNATURES FOR PARTY CANDIDATES
Idaho	Idaho Code Ann. § 34	Political party: • Senate: $500 • House: $300 Can use signatures instead of fees Independent: None	Senate: 1,000 House: 500
Illinois	ILCS Ch. 10, ACT 5, art. VII	None	Major party: • Senate: 5,000—fixed by statute • House: 0.5% of qualified party primary voters in the district
Indiana	Ind. Code Ann. § 3–8	None	Senate: At least 4,500 signatures, including a minimum of 500 signatures from each of the state's congressional districts. House: Declaration of candidacy only

SIGNATURE REQUIREMENTS FOR INDEPENDENT CANDIDATES	WHERE TO SUBMIT SIGNATURES/ FORMS	NOTES
Senate: 1,000 House: 500	Idaho secretary of state	Independent: Must file a C1 "Appointment and Certification of Political Treasurer" form with the Idaho secretary of state. The candidate must file this form prior to announcing his or her candidacy, accepting donations, or spending money on the campaign.
Independent: • Senate: 1% of voters or 25,000 voters, whichever is fewer • House: 5% of voters who voted at the last general election in the district	Nomination papers go to the Illinois State Board of Elections. Statement of economic interests must be filed with the Illinois secretary of state.	Multiple filing requirements including address, political affiliation, office being sought, and paper including economic interests.
Senate: Signatures from registered voters equal to 2% of the total votes cast for secretary of state in the last election. House: Registered voters equal to 2% of the total votes cast for secretary of state in the last election in the congressional district the candidate seeks to represent.	Indiana Election Division	Libertarian candidates must file with the Libertarian Party and be nominated at a convention. No signature requirements for them.

STATE	STATE STATUTE	FEES	SIGNATURES FOR PARTY CANDIDATES
Iowa	Iowa Code Ann. Tit. 2, Subt. 1	None	Senate: At least 1% of the voters of the candidate's party, in each of at least 10 counties in the state, and in the aggregate not less than 0.5% of the total vote of the candidate's party in the state, as shown in the last general election House: At least 2% of the voters of the candidate's party, as shown by the last general election, in each of at least one-half of the counties of the district, and in the aggregate not less than 1% of the total vote of the candidate's party in such district, as shown by the last general election
Kansas	Kan. Stat. Ann. Ch. 25, Art. 1–3	1% of the office's annual salary Can be paid in lieu of the signatures for major party only	Senate: 1% of the state's current voter registration total of the party House: Signatures must equal at least 2% of the district's current voter registration total of the party
Kentucky	Ky. Rev. Stat. Ann. tit. X, Ch. 118	$500	Only 2 signatures required for Dem/Rep candidates

SIGNATURE REQUIREMENTS FOR INDEPENDENT CANDIDATES	WHERE TO SUBMIT SIGNATURES/ FORMS	NOTES
A candidate who is not affiliated with any political party or nonparty political organizations (NPPO) can be nominated by petition. NPPOs nominate and select their own candidates. True independents can run with petitions. Senate: 1,500 collected from at least 10 counties House: 375 from the congressional district	Iowa secretary of state	If a political party fails to nominate a candidate at the primary election, the party may hold a convention after the primary to nominate a candidate. NPPOs are permitted to hold conventions to nominate their candidates but have a specific set of rules on how to qualify.
Senate: At least 5,000 House: 4% of the current total of qualified voters in the district as determined by the Kansas secretary of state	Kansas secretary of state Kansas Governmental Ethics Commission	Independents must meet signature requirements. Candidates must also register with the ethics commission.
Senate: 5,000 House: 400	Kentucky secretary of state	Party candidates gain ballot access by nomination or winning the primary, as there are only 2 signatures required for major party candidates. A candidate defeated at the primary election is not permitted to run in the general election. The candidate must file a notification of candidacy and declaration form.

STATE	STATE STATUTE	FEES	SIGNATURES FOR PARTY CANDIDATES
Louisiana	La. Stat. Ann. § T. 18,	$900	None
Maine	Me. Rev. Stat. tit. 21-A, Ch. 5, Subch. 3, art. 4.	None	Senate: At least 2,000 signatures, but no more than 3,000 House: At least 1,000 signatures, but no more than 1,500
Maryland	Md. Code Ann., Elec. Law tit. 5	Senate: $290 House: $100	None

SIGNATURE REQUIREMENTS FOR INDEPENDENT CANDIDATES	WHERE TO SUBMIT SIGNATURES/ FORMS	NOTES
None	File with Louisiana secretary of state. Must also file a notice of candidacy. Includes name, affirmation of qualifications, financial information, voter registration, address, etc.	In Louisiana, all candidates, regardless of party affiliation, run in the general election. If a candidate receives a majority of the vote in the general election, he or she wins outright. If no candidate meets that threshold, a runoff election is held between the top two receiving the most votes.
Senate: At least 4,000 signatures, but no more than 6,000 House: At least 2,000 signatures, but no more than 3,000	Verified by the registrar of voters or municipal clerk in the munici-pality where the signatures were collected. Then submitted to the Maine secretary of state.	Must submit a "Consent of Candidate" form or a "Nonparty Candidate's Consent" form if an independent.
Lesser of 10,000 registered voters or 1% of the eligible voters for the district	Maryland State Board of Elections Financial disclosure form to Maryland State Ethics Commission	Must also file a Certificate of Candidacy, Statement of Organization, and Financial Disclosure Form.

STATE	STATE STATUTE	FEES	SIGNATURES FOR PARTY CANDIDATES
Massachusetts	Mass. Gen. Laws Ann. Pt. I, tit. VIII, Ch. 53	None	Senate (all parties): 10,000 House (all parties): 2,000
Michigan	Mich. Comp. Laws Ann. § 168.544c	None	Partisan primary: • Senate: 15,000, with at least 100 signatures coming from each of at least half of the state's congressional districts • House: 1,000
Minnesota	Minn. Stat. Ann. § 204B	Partisan: • Senate: $400 • House: $300 Independent: $0	Instead of fees: • Senate: 2,000 • House: 1,000

SIGNATURE REQUIREMENTS FOR INDEPENDENT CANDIDATES	WHERE TO SUBMIT SIGNATURES/ FORMS	NOTES
Senate (all parties): 10,000 House (all parties): 2,000	Nomination papers (with the signatures) to the secretary of the commonwealth	At least one of the certified nomination papers must contain a written acceptance of nomination personally signed by either the candidate or his or her authorized attorney. A nonparty candidate must file a certificate proving that he or she is a registered voter and is not part of a recognized political party.
Senate: 30,000 House: 3,000	Michigan secretary of state	Political parties are defined as those whose principal candidate received at least 5% of the total votes cast for all candidates for Michigan secretary of state in the last election. Additionally, you need an affidavit of identity.
Senate: Signatures must equal either 1% of the total number of individuals who voted in the state at the last preceding state general election, or 2,000, whichever is less House: Signatures must equal either 5% of the total number of individuals who voted in the district at the last preceding state general election, or 1,000, whichever is less	Affidavit of candidacy and nominating petition to Minnesota secretary of state	Instead of running under a political party, an independent candidate may designate a nonrecognized party or political principle.

STATE	STATE STATUTE	FEES	SIGNATURES FOR PARTY CANDIDATES
Mississippi	Miss. Code. Ann. Tit. 23 Ch. 15	Party Senate: $1,000 Party House: $500	None for major party candidates
Missouri	Mo. Ann. Stat. tit. IX, Ch. 115	Partisan candidate: • Senate: $200 • House: $100 Independent: None	None for partisan candidates
Montana	Mont. Code Ann. Tit. 13	1% of the salary for the office being sought	None
Nebraska	Neb. Rev. Stat. Ann. Ch. 32	1% of the office's annual salary	4,000 signatures for candidates for statewide office of US House
Nevada	Nev. Rev. Stat. Ann. tit. 24, Ch. 293	Senate: $500 House: $300	None

SIGNATURE REQUIREMENTS FOR INDEPENDENT CANDIDATES	WHERE TO SUBMIT SIGNATURES/ FORMS	NOTES
Senate: At least 1,000 signatures House: At least 200 signatures	Mississippi secretary of state	Petitions for candidacy must also include a qualifying statement of intent that includes, address, party, and office being sought.
Independent: • Senate: 0.5% of the total number of votes cast in the state for the office being sought at the last election • House: 2% of all voters who voted for the specific office in the last election	Missouri Department of Revenue Elections Division of the Office of the secretary of state	A candidate must also file an affidavit with the Missouri Department of Revenue affirming that the candidate is not behind on any state-owed taxes.
At least 5% of the total votes cast at the last general election for the successful candidate for the office being sought	Montana secretary of state	All candidates must file an "Path of Candidacy," an indigent candidate declaration, and petition of nomination.
10% of the total number of registered voters voting for governor or president at the most recent general election; not to exceed 2,000	Nebraska secretary of state	Every prospective candidate must complete and submit a candidate filing form.
Independent: 1% of the total votes cast at the last general election for the same office the candidate seeks OR Senate: 250 signatures House: 100 registered voters' signatures None for minor party.	Nevada secretary of state	Major party candidates are nominated via primary election. Minor parties must file a list of candidates with the Nevada secretary of state before any minor party candidates can file individually. Independent candidates may only run in the general election.

STATE	STATE STATUTE	FEES	SIGNATURES FOR PARTY CANDIDATES
New Hampshire	N.H. Rev. Stat. Ann. tit. LXIII, Ch. 655	House: $50 Senate: $100	Senate: 200 House: 100
New Jersey	N.J. Stat. Ann. tit. 19	None	Senate: 1,000 House: 200
New Mexico	N.M. Stat. Ann. Ch.1 Art. 8	None	Must first submit signatures: at least equal to or greater than the following number of voters, whichever is greater: for statewide offices, 230 voters; and for congressional candidates, 77 voters. Every candidate receiving at least 20% of the vote at the party convention will be certified to the New Mexico secretary of state as a convention-designated nominee for that office by the political party.
New York	N.Y. Elec. Law § Ch. 17, art. 6	None	House: 5% of the number of active enrolled voters in the district. Senate: 5% of the number of active enrolled voters in the state. If the amount is fixed by statute, it is the lesser amount of 5% or the statute.

SIGNATURE REQUIREMENTS FOR INDEPENDENT CANDIDATES	WHERE TO SUBMIT SIGNATURES/ FORMS	NOTES
Senate: 3,000 House: 1,500	New Hampshire secretary of state	Candidates must also file a declaration of intent.
Senate: 800 House: 100	New Jersey secretary of state	An independent candidate must submit the same paper-work as a partisan candidate. All candidates must sign a "Certificate of Acceptance" and an "Oath of Allegiance."
Independent Senate: 3% of the total number of votes cast for governor in the previous general election. Independent House: 3% of the total number of votes cast for governor in the previous general election in that district. Minor party: signatures of at least 1% of the total number of the votes cast at the last preceding general election for the office of governor.	New Mexico secretary of state	Rules vary according to each minor party, but minor party candidates usually obtain ballot access through nomination.
Signatures equaling at least 5% of the total number of votes cast for governor within the political unit at the last gubernatorial election, or a fixed total established by statute, whichever is less.	New York State Board of Elections	If the congressional district is entirely within New York City, the petition must be filed with the city Board of Elections. If the district of the office being sought comprises more than one county, the petition must be filed with the New York State Board of Elections.

STATE	STATE STATUTE	FEES	SIGNATURES FOR PARTY CANDIDATES
North Carolina	N.C. Gen. Stat. Ann. § Ch. 163, Subch. V	1% of the office's annual salary	None
North Dakota	N.D. Cent. Code Ann. § 16.1–11	None	Senate: 300 House: 300
Ohio	Ohio Rev. Code Ann. tit. XXXV, Ch. 3513	Senator: $150 House: $85	Senator: 1,000 qualified electors who are members of the same political party as the candidate House: 50 qualified electors who are members of the same political party as the candidate
Oklahoma	Okla. Stat. Ann. tit. 26, Ch. A1	Senator: $2000 House: $1000 Can petition with signatures instead of fee	4% of registered voters who will be eligible to vote for the candidate in the election

SIGNATURE REQUIREMENTS FOR INDEPENDENT CANDIDATES	WHERE TO SUBMIT SIGNATURES/ FORMS	NOTES
Write-in candidates: • Senate: 500 • House: 250 Independent candidates: • Senate: 1.5% of the total number of voters who voted in the most recent election for governor • House: 1.5% of the total number of registered voters in the district as of January 1 of the election year	North Carolina State Board of Elections	North Carolina is one of the most recent states to reform and amend their election process requirements to mirror reasonable requirements similar to other jurisdictions.
Senate: 1,000 House: 1,000	North Dakota secretary of state, Elections Division	Affidavit of candidacy and a statement of interests must be filed along with signatures for all candidates.
Senate: 5,000 qualified electors House: If 5,000 or more electors voted for the office of governor in the most recent election, 1% of electors; if less than 5,000 electors voted for said office, 5% of the vote or 25, whichever is less	Ohio secretary of state	Statement of candidacy required, to be filed with secretary of state. Filing fees apply for all candidates and must be paid in addition to petition requirements.
4% of registered voters who will be eligible to vote for the candidate in the election	Oklahoma State Election Board	Process same for all candidates

STATE	STATE STATUTE	FEES	SIGNATURES FOR PARTY CANDIDATES
Oregon	Or. Rev. Stat. Ann. tit. 23, Ch. 249	Senate: $150 House: $100 Minor/independent: No fee	Instead of paying the filing fee, a candidate may file a nominating petition with the required number of signatures: • House: The lesser of 1,000 signatures or 2% of the number of votes cast in the district for president by members of the candidate's party. • Senate: The lesser of 1,000 signatures or 2% of the number of votes cast for president by members of the candidate's party.
Pennsylvania	Pa. Stat. and Cons. Stat. Ann. tit. 25 P.S., Ch. 14, art. 9	Senate: $200 House: $100	Senate: 2,000 House: 1,000
Rhode Island	R.I. Gen. Laws Ann. § 17–14	None	House: 500 Senate: 1,000
South Carolina	S.C. Code Ann. Tit. 7, Ch. 11	2% of the office's salary	None

SIGNATURE REQUIREMENTS FOR INDEPENDENT CANDIDATES	WHERE TO SUBMIT SIGNATURES/ FORMS	NOTES
Partisan: • Senate: 1% of votes cast in the state for president • House: 1% of votes cast in the district for president Unaffiliated: • Senate: 1,000 signatures obtained at the assembly • House: 500 signatures obtained at the assembly	Oregon secretary of state	An unaffiliated candidate must submit a candidate filing form to the secretary of state and then organize an assembly. There are then procedures about how the assembly of registered voters can nominate independent candidates.
2% of the largest entire vote cast for an elected candidate in the last election within the district/state	Pennsylvania secretary of state	Note: On February 19, 2018, the Pennsylvania Supreme Court adopted a new congressional district map after ruling that the original map constituted illegal gerrymander. District locations and numbers were changed by the new map.
Senate: 1,000 House: 500	Rhode Island secretary of state	Same filing procedure for all candidates.
5% of the qualified registered electors in the geographical area of the office being sought. No petition candidate is required to collect more than 10,000 signatures for any office.	South Carolina State Election Commission	Candidates must file a "Statement of Intention of Candidacy/Party Pledge Form" and a statement of economic interests.

STATE	STATE STATUTE	FEES	SIGNATURES FOR PARTY CANDIDATES
South Dakota	S.D. Codified Laws tit. 12, Ch. 12–6, Ch 12–7	None	Senate: lesser of 50 voters or 1% of the party's total registered members House: 1% of the party's total registered members in the applicable electoral district
Tennessee	Tenn. Code Ann. Tit. 2	None	25 signatures
Texas	Tex. Elec. Code Ann. Tit. 9	Senate: $5,000 House: $3,125 Signatures can be used in lieu of the filing fee.	Major party • Senate: 5,000 • House: 2% of the district or 500.
Utah	Utah Code Ann. § 20A-9	$50 plus 1/8 of 1% of the total salary for the full term of the office.	Senate: 28,000 House: 7,000

SIGNATURE REQUIREMENTS FOR INDEPENDENT CANDIDATES	WHERE TO SUBMIT SIGNATURES/ FORMS	NOTES
House: 1% of the total combined vote cast for governor at the last certified gubernatorial election within the district or political subdivision	County auditor or the South Dakota secretary of state	Only independents or nonparty affiliated voters may sign the petition for an independent candidate.
25 signatures	Tennessee secretary of state, Division of Elections	Candidates must also obtain a nominating petition from a county election commission office or the office of the state coordinator of elections.
State-qualified minor parties nominate candidates by convention. Independent: • Senate: 1% of all votes cast for governor in the last election • House: 5% of all votes cast for governor in the district in the last election	Texas secretary of state	In order to run with a major political party, a candidate must file an application with the county or state party chair. An independent candidate must file a declaration of intent with the county judge of their district or the Texas secretary of state.
Senate: Petition with the signatures of at least 1,000 registered Utah voters House: Petition with at least 300 signatures within the congressional district, or at least 5% of the registered voters residing within the congressional district, whichever is less	Petitions go to the Office of the Utah Lieutenant Governor	Requires a declaration of candidacy in person with either the Office of the Utah Lieutenant Governor or the county clerk in the candidate's county of residence. Also need a fair campaign practices pledge.

STATE	STATE STATUTE	FEES	SIGNATURES FOR PARTY CANDIDATES
Vermont	Vt. Stat. Ann. tit. 17, Ch. 49	None	500 signatures
Virginia	VA Code Ann. T. 24.2, Ch. 5,	None	Senate: 10,000, including 400 qualified voters from each congressional district House: 1,000
Washington	Wash. Rev. Code Ann. § 29A.24	1% of the annual salary of the office at the time of filing.	In lieu of paying a filing fee, candidates can submit a filing fee petition with a number of signatures equivalent to the dollar amount of the filing fee for the specific office.

SIGNATURE REQUIREMENTS FOR INDEPENDENT CANDIDATES	WHERE TO SUBMIT SIGNATURES/ FORMS	NOTES
500 signatures	Vermont secretary of state	A party committee nominates the candidate for a minor political party in the general election. The candidate must file a candidate consent form and party committee nomination. Independent candidates in the general election must file a statement of nomination form and candidate consent form.
Senate: 10,000, including 400 qualified voters from each congressional district House: 1,000	Virginia State Board of Elections	A political party and independent candidate both must complete the candidate qualification certificate form. The form is a written statement (made under oath) indicating that the candidate is qualified to vote for and to hold the office.
In lieu of paying a filing fee, candidates can submit a filing fee petition with a number of signatures equivalent to the dollar amount of the filing fee for the specific office.	Washington secretary of state and the Washington Public Disclosure Commission	The candidate must do the following on the application of candidacy: • Declare that he or she is a registered voter within the jurisdiction of the office for which he or she is filing (the candidate must include the address at which he or she is registered) • Indicate the position for which he or she is filing

STATE	STATE STATUTE	FEES	SIGNATURES FOR PARTY CANDIDATES
Washington (cont.)			
West Virginia	W. Va. Code, Ch. 3, Art. 5.	1% of annual salary for the position	None
Wisconsin	Wis. Stat. Ann. § Ch. 8	None	Senate: 2,000–4,000 House: 1,000–2,000
Wyoming	Wyo. Stat. Ann. § 22–5	$200 fixed fee for all	Major party: None

SIGNATURE REQUIREMENTS FOR INDEPENDENT CANDIDATES	WHERE TO SUBMIT SIGNATURES/ FORMS	NOTES
		• State a party preference, if the office is a partisan office • Indicate the amount of the filing fee (the candidate may also indicate that he or she is filing a petition in lieu of the filing fee) • Sign the declaration of candidacy, stating that the information provided on the form is true and swearing or affirming that he or she will support the Constitution and laws of the United States and the constitution and laws of the state of Washington
Independent Senate: 1% of all votes cast in the last election for the office being sought Independent House: 1% of all votes cast in the last election for the office being sought	West Virginia secretary of state	The candidate must also file a financial disclosure statement with the West Virginia Ethics Commission within 10 days of filing the certificate of announcement.
Senate: 2,000–4,000 House: 1,000–2,000	Wisconsin Elections Commission	Must file a declaration of candidacy with the Wisconsin Elections Commission.
2% of all votes cast for US representative in the last election (about 4,025)	Wyoming secretary of state	The application of nomination goes to the secretary of state

Notes

Introduction

1. Cynthia McFadden, William M. Arkin, Kevin Monahan, and Ken Dilanian, "U.S. Intel: Russia Compromised Seven States Prior to 2016 Election," NBC News, February 28, 2018, https://www.nbcnews.com/politics/elections/u-s-intel-russia-compromised-seven-states-prior-2016-election-n850296.
2. Victoria Bassetti, *Electoral Dysfunction* (New York: New Press, 2012), 55–60.

Part I: Voting State by State: What You Need to Know *Now*

1. "Failure to Vote," Western Australian Electoral Commission, https://www.elections.wa.gov.au/vote/failure-vote; Tacey Rychter, "How Compulsory Voting Works: Australians Explain," *New York Times*, October 22, 2018, https://www.nytimes.com/2018/10/22/world/australia/compulsory-voting.html (quoting Neil Ennis, Lawnton, Queensland); Drew DeSilver, "U.S. Trails Most Developed Countries in Voter Turnout," Pew Research Center, May 21, 2018, https://www.pewresearch.org/fact-tank/2018/05/21/u-s-voter-turnout-trails-most-developed-countries/. *See generally* Organization for Economic Cooperation and Development, http://www.oecd.org/about/.
2. Robert Schlesinger, "The Size of the U.S. and the World in 2016," *U.S. News and World Report*, January 5, 2016, https://www.usnews.com/opinion/blogs/robert-schlesinger/articles/2016-01-05/us-population-in-2016-according-to-census-estimates-322-762-018; DeSilver, "U.S. Trails Most Developed Countries in Voter Turnout."
3. Rychter, "How Compulsory Voting Works: Australians Explain"; DeSilver, "U.S. Trails Most Developed Countries in Voter Turnout."
4. Sean McElwee, Brian Schaffner, and Jesse Rhodes, "How Oregon Increased Voter Turnout More Than Any Other State," *Nation*, July 27, 2017,

https://www.thenation.com/article/how-oregon-increased-voter-turnout-more-than-any-other-state/.

Chapter 1: The Two-Step "Recipe" for Voting

1. *See generally* "Moving and Registering to Vote," US Election Assistance Commission, accessed May 5, 2019, https://www.eac.gov/voters/voter-faqs#I've-moved-recently.-Can-I-still-vote?
2. "Register to Vote or Update Your Information," Florida Department of State, 2019, https://dos.myflorida.com/elections/for-voters/voter-registration/register-to-vote-or-update-your-information/; "Same-day voter registration," Ballotpedia, accessed April 3, 2019, https://ballotpedia.org/Same-day_voter_registration.
3. "About The National Voter Registration Act," US Department of Justice, updated May 21, 2019, https://www.justice.gov/crt/about-national-voter-registration-act.
4. "Voter Registration Form," Rock the Vote, accessed October 26, 2019, https://www.rockthevote.org/register-to-vote/.
5. Another resource with relatively comprehensive fifty-state information is offered by the National Conference of State Legislatures at www.ncsl.org.
6. "Absentee and Early Voting," USA.gov, May 21, 2019, https://www.usa.gov/absentee-voting.
7. Pub. L. 107–252, codified at 52 U.S.C. §§ 20901–21145. *See generally* "Help America Vote Act," U.S. Election Assistance Commission, accessed May 5, 2019, https://www.eac.gov/about/help-america-vote-act/.
8. "Provisional Ballots," National Conference of State Legislatures, October 15, 2018, http://www.ncsl.org/research/elections-and-campaigns/provisional-ballots.aspx (listing differences in provisional voting procedures by state).
9. "Absentee and Early Voting."

Chapter 2: Moving Out of State, Missed an Election Cycle, or Off to College? An "Ingredient" List for Staying Registered

1. *See generally* "Register and Vote in Your State," US Election Assistance Commission, https://www.eac.gov/voters/register-and-vote-in-your-state/.
2. "Voting in College," Best Colleges, accessed October 26, 2019, https://www.bestcolleges.com/resources/voting-in-college/.
3. Trip Gabriel, "Virginia Official Pulls Republican's Name from Bowl to Pick Winner of Tied Race," *New York Times*, January 4, 2018, https://www.nytimes.com/2018/01/04/us/virginia-tie.html.

Chapter 3: The Latest on Ballot Confusion and Voting Machine Clunkery

1. Dana Chisnell and Whitney Quesenbery, "How a Badly Designed Ballot Might Have Swayed the Election in Florida," *Washington Post*, November 12, 2018, https://www.washingtonpost.com/outlook/2018/11/12/how-badly-designed-ballot-might-have-swayed-election-florida/; Ron Elving, "The Florida Recount of 2000: A Nightmare That Goes On Haunting," NPR, November 12, 2018, https://www.npr.org/2018/11/12/666812854/the-florida-recount-of-2000-a-nightmare-that-goes-on-haunting.
2. Lawrence Norden and Andrea Córdova McCadney, "Voting Machines at Risk: Where We Stand Today," Brennan Center for Justice, March 5, 2019, https://www.brennancenter.org/analysis/voting-machines-risk-where-we-stand-today.
3. Andrew Cohen, "No One in America Should Have to Wait 7 Hours to Vote," November 5, 2012, *Atlantic*, https://www.theatlantic.com/politics/archive/2012/11/no-one-in-america-should-have-to-wait-7-hours-to-vote/264506/.
4. Erik Larson and Margaret Newkirk, "Kemp's Office Blames Georgia Voter Lines on Lengthy Ballot," Bloomberg, November 6, 2018, https://www.bloomberg.com/news/articles/2018-11-06/kemp-s-office-blames-long-georgia-voter-lines-on-lengthy-ballot.
5. Pam Fessler, "Questions and Answers on Voting Rules," NPR, October 10, 2008, https://www.npr.org/templates/story/story.php?storyId=95573939.
6. Pam Fessler, "Voters with Disabilities Fight for More Accessible Polling Place," NPR, October 24, 2016, https://www.npr.org/2016/10/24/499177544/disabled-voters-fight-for-more-accessible-polling-places.
7. "The Blind Voter Experience: A Comparison of the 2008, 2012, 2014, 2016 and 2018 Elections," National Federation of the Blind, January 2018 (on file with author).
8. 42 U.S.C. §§ 12101, 1973ee-1973ee-6; Pub. L. 107–252.
9. "Voters with Disabilities: Challenges to Voting Accessibility," US Government Accountability Office, April 23, 2013, https://www.gao.gov/products/GAO-13-538SP.
10. "10 Tips for Voters with Disabilities," US Election Assistance Commission, November 2015, https://www.aapd.com/wp-content/uploads/2017/04/10-Tips-for-Voters-with-Disabilities-EAC.pdf.
11. "Voting Rights Act Section 203 Determinations," US Census Bureau, October 12, 2011, https://www.census.gov/2010census/news/pdf/20111011_203slides.pdf; D'Vera Cohn, "More Voters Will Have Access to Non-English Ballots in the Next Election Cycle," Pew Research Center, De-

cember 16, 2016, https://www.pewresearch.org/fact-tank/2016/12/16/more-voters-will-have-access-to-non-english-ballots-in-the-next-election-cycle/; Kristen Clarke and Ezra Rosenberg, "Trump Administration Has Voting Rights Act on Life Support," CNN, August 6, 2018, https://www.cnn.com/2018/08/06/opinions/voting-rights-act-anniversary-long-way-to-go-clarke-rosenberg-opinion/index.html.

Chapter 4: What Does the "Right" to Vote Even Mean?

1. The first ten amendments comprise the Bill of Rights, amendments that were added in 1791 (to include religion, speech, bearing arms, quartering of soldiers, search and seizure, grand jury, double jeopardy, self-incrimination, due process, rights of accused in criminal prosecutions, jury trial, excessive bail, cruel and unusual punishment, non-enumerated rights, and rights reserved to the states). More amendments followed:

    in 1795 (suits against a state)
    in 1804 (election of president and vice president)
    in 1865 (abolition of slavery and involuntary servitude)
    in 1868 (due process for states and equal protection, among other things)
    in 1870 (voting rights)
    in 1913 (federal income tax and popular election of senators)
    in 1919 (prohibition)
    in 1920 (women's right to vote)
    in 1933 (commencement of a presidential term and succession)
    in 1933 (repeal of prohibition)
    in 1951 (two-term limit on the president)
    in 1961 (District of Columbia presidential vote)
    in 1964 (abolition of poll tax requirement in federal elections)
    in 1967 (presidential vacancy, disability, and inability)
    in 1971 (right to vote at age 18)
    in 1992 (congressional compensation).

    See "Amendment Summary: 27 Updates to the U.S. Constitution," United States History, https://www.u-s-history.com/pages/h926.html.
2. "The House of Representatives shall be composed of Members chosen every second Year *by the People of the several States*." (Emphasis added.)
3. "The Times, Places, and Manner of holding Elections for Senators and Representatives, shall be prescribed in each State by the Legislature thereof."
4. District of Columbia v. Heller, 554 U.S. 570 (2009).
5. "Representatives shall be apportioned among the several States according

to their respective numbers, counting *the whole number of persons* in each State." (Emphasis added.)

6. "The right to vote shall not be denied or abridged by the United States or by any State on account of race, color, or previous condition of servitude."
7. "The Senate of the United States shall be composed of two Senators from each States, *elected by the people thereof*, for six years; and each Senator shall have one vote." (Emphasis added.)
8. George H. Haynes, *The Senate of the United States* (Boston: Houghton Mifflin, 1938), 103–16.
9. NCC staff, "The Day the Constitution Was Ratified," National Constitution Center, June 21, 2019, https://constitutioncenter.org/blog/the-day-the-constitution-was-ratified; Kat Eschner, "For a Few Decades in the 18th Century, Women and African-Americans Could Vote in New Jersey," *Smithsonian Magazine*, November 16, 2017, https://www.smithsonianmag.com/smart-news/why-black-people-and-women-lost-vote-new-jersey-180967186/ (citing Judith Apter Klinghoffer and Lois Elkis, "'The Petticoat Electors': Women's Suffrage in New Jersey, 1776–1807," *Journal of the Early Republic* [1992]).
10. "The Twenty-Third Amendment, 1961," Smithsonian National Museum of American History, https://americanhistory.si.edu/democracy-exhibition/vote-voice/getting-vote/sometimes-it-takes-amendment/twenty-0.
11. "The right of citizens of the United States to vote in any primary or other election for President or Vice President, for electors [i.e., members of the Electoral College] for President or Vice President, or for Senator or Representative in Congress, shall not be denied or bridged by the United States or any State by reason of failure to pay poll tax or other tax."
12. Deborah N. Archer and Derek T. Muller, "The Twenty-Fourth Amendment," National Constitution Center, https://constitutioncenter.org/interactive-constitution/amendments/amendment-xxiv.
13. 400 U.S. 112 (1970); *see also* Jocelyn Benson and Michael T. Morley, "The Twenty-Sixth Amendment," National Constitution Center, https://constitutioncenter.org/interactive-constitution/amendments/amendment-xxvi.
14. "The right of the citizens of the United States, who are eighteen years of age or older, to vote shall not be denied or abridged by the United States or by any State on account of age."
15. Yick Wo v. Hopkins, 118 U.S. 356 (1886).
16. Reynolds v. Sims, 377 U.S. 533 (1964).

Chapter 5: Who Gets to Vote Legally in America

1. Tashijian v. Republican Party of Connecticut, 479 U.S. 208, 227 (1986).
2. Ibid., at 228–29.
3. 107 Stat. 77, 52 U.S.C. §§ 20501–20511.
4. *See generally* "The National Voter Registration Act of 1993 (NVRA)," US Department of Justice, August 7, 2017, https://www.justice.gov/crt/national-voter-registration-act-1993-nvra.
5. *See, e.g.,* Condon v. Reno, 913 F. Supp. 946 (D.S.C. 1995).
6. Pub. L. 104–208, 110 Stat. 3009, codified in scattered sections of 8 U.S.C. Ch. 12.
7. Jamin B. Raskin, "Legal Aliens, Local Citizens: The Historical, Constitutional, and Theoretical Meanings of Alien Suffrage," *University of Pennsylvania Law Review* 141, no. 4 (April 1993): 1409–10; Ronald Hayduk, *Democracy for All: Restoring Immigrant Voting Rights in the United States* (New York: Routledge, 2006), 87–100.
8. Jennine Miller and Peter Gonzales, "'I Matter! I Vote!': Overcoming the Disenfranchisement of Homeless and Formerly Homeless Voters," *Temple Political & Civil Rights Law Review* 11, no. 2 (Spring 2002): 348.
9. Sean McElwee, "The Income Gap at the Polls: The Right Aren't Just Megadonors. They're Also Dominating the Voting Booth," *Politico*, January 7, 2015, https://www.politico.com/magazine/story/2015/01/income-gap-at-the-polls-113997.
10. "Voting Rights Restoration," Brennan Center for Justice, https://www.brennancenter.org/issues/restoring-voting-rights.
11. Seema Jayachandran, "Unable to Post Bail? You Will Pay for That for Many Years," *New York Times*, March 1, 2019, https://www.nytimes.com/2019/03/01/business/cash-bail-system-reform.html.
12. Marc Mauer, "Voting Behind Bars: An Argument for Voting by Prisoners," *Howard Law Journal* 54, no. 3 (Spring 2011): 551.
13. Michael Levy, "United States Presidential Election of 2000," *Encyclopedia Britannica*, accessed May 5, 2019, https://www.britannica.com/event/United-States-presidential-election-of-2000; German Lopez, "Florida's Bill Nelson Would Have Likely Beat Rick Scott If Ex-Felons Had Been Able to Vote," Vox, November 19, 2018, https://www.vox.com/policy-and-politics/2018/11/19/18102579/florida-senate-midterm-election-results-felons-nelson-scott; Terri Hallenbeck, "After Second Recount, Ainsworth Defeats Buxton by One Vote," *Seven Days*, December 14, 2016, https://www.sevendaysvt.com/OffMessage/archives/2016/12/14/after-second-recount

-ainsworth-defeats-buxton-by-one-vote; Tim Meko, Denise Lu, and Lazaro Gamio, "How Trump Won the Presidency with Razor-Thin Margins in Swing States," *Washington Post*, November 11, 2016, https://www.washingtonpost.com/graphics/politics/2016-election/swing-state-margins/.

CHAPTER 6: Key Ingredients to Electing a President (and What's the Electoral College, Anyway?)

1. *See* Perkins v. Elg, 307 U.S. 325, 328 (1939) (holding that a child born in the United States of alien parentage becomes a citizen).
2. Philip Bump, "How to Run for President, in 4 Easy Steps," *Washington Post*, February 23, 2015, https://www.washingtonpost.com/news/the-fix/wp/2015/02/23/how-to-run-for-president-in-4-easy-steps/?utm_term=.b1877f8189fa. *See also* "New Statements of Candidacy," Federal Election Commission, accessed June 3, 2019. See also https://webforms.fec.gov/webforms/form2/index.htm (prompting process for filing a Form 2).
3. "Ballot Access for Presidential Candidates," Ballotpedia, https://ballotpedia.org/Ballot_access_for_presidential_candidates.
4. Quynh Uong, "The 8 Worst Ballot Access Laws in America," *IVN*, August 1, 2018, https://ivn.us/2018/08/01/8-worst-ballot-access-laws-america.
5. Daniel P. Tokaji, *Election Law in a Nutshell* (St. Paul, MN: West Academic Publishing, 2015), 265.
6. California Democratic Party v. Jones, 530 U.S. 567 (2000).
7. *See* John C. Fortier et al., "2018 Primary Election Turnout and Reforms," Bipartisan Policy Center, November 2018, https://bipartisanpolicy.org/wp-content/uploads/2019/03/2018-Primary-Election-Turnout-and-Reforms.pdf, page 12.
8. "Caucus FAQ," Republican Party of Iowa, https://www.iowagop.org/caucus-faq/.
9. "How Do Caucuses Work?," howstuffworks, https://people.howstuffworks.com/question7211.htm.
10. Peter H. Aranson, *American Government: Strategy and Choice* (Cambridge, MA: Winthrop Publishers, 1981), 161.
11. Rebecca Shabad, "Who Gets to Be a Delegate at the Presidential Nominating Conventions?," CBS News, March 21, 2016, https://www.cbsnews.com/news/who-gets-to-be-a-delegate-at-the-presidential-nominating-conventions/ (quoting Ben Ginsberg, a lawyer for the 2016 Republican campaign for president).

12. Elaine Kamarck, "What Is a Brokered Convention, and Are We Going to Have One in 2016?," Brookings, March 12, 2016, https://www.brookings.edu/blog/fixgov/2016/03/12/what-is-a-brokered-convention-and-are-we-going-to-have-one-in-2016/; Diana Pearl, "All About Super Delegates, the Electoral College and How Trump Can Clinch Nomination Before California Even Votes," *People*, May 9, 2016, https://people.com/celebrity/presidential-election-2016-how-the-electoral-college-and-superdelegates-work/.
13. Paul Bedard, "2018: Democrats Lead GOP by 12 Million Registered Voters, 40% D, 29% R, 28% I," *Washington Examiner*, July 13, 2018, https://www.washingtonexaminer.com/washington-secrets/2018-democrats-lead-gop-by-12-million-registered-voters.
14. "Electoral College Fast Facts," Office of the Historian, United States House of Representatives, accessed June 9, 2019, https://history.house.gov/Institution/Electoral-College/Electoral-College/; "What is the Electoral College?," Office of the Federal Register, US National Archives and Records Administration, https://www.archives.gov/federal-register/electoral-college/about.html. The faithless electors issue is currently pending before the US Supreme Court. Nina Totenberg, "Supreme Court to Hear Faithless Electors' Case," NPS, January 17, 2020, https://www.npr.org/2020/01/17/797472072/supreme-court-to-hear-faithless-electors-case.
15. "Distribution of Electoral Votes," US National Archives and Records Administration, accessed October 27, 2019, https://www.archives.gov/federal-register/electoral-college/allocation.html.
16. Monica Busch, "Experts Explain How 2020 Swing States Will Be Determined," *Bustle*, May 22, 2019, https://www.bustle.com/p/experts-explain-how-2020-swing-states-will-be-determined-17029006; Adam Wollner, "'The New Swing States': Presidential Battleground Map Shifts Heading into 2020," McClatchy, December 12, 2018, https://www.mcclatchydc.com/news/politics-government/election/campaigns/article222917745.html.
17. Merrit Kennedy, "ACLU Sues Over Florida Law That Requires Felons to Pay Fees, Fines Before Voting," NPR, July 1, 2019, https://www.npr.org/2019/07/01/737668646/aclu-sues-over-florida-law-that-requires-felons-to-pay-fees-fines-before-voting.
18. U.S. Const., Article II, Section 1, Clause. 2.
19. "About the Electors," US National Archives and Records Administration, accessed October 27, 2019, https://www.archives.gov/federal-register/electoral-college/electors.html.
20. Bush v. Gore, 531 U.S. 98 (2000); "This Day in History, January 6: Con-

gress Certifies Bush the Winner of 2000 Elections," History.com, last modified June 14, 2019, https://www.history.com/this-day-in-history/congress-certifies-bush-winner-of-2000-elections.

21. McPherson v. Blacker, 141 U.S. 1, 10 (1892).
22. Danielle Kurtzleben, "How to Win the Presidency with 23 Percent of the Popular Vote," NPR, November 2, 2016, https://www.npr.org/2016/11/02/500112248/how-to-win-the-presidency-with-27-percent-of-the-popular-vote.
23. Dante Chinni and Sally Bronston, "New Election Map: Ohio, Colorado No Longer Swing States," NBC News, November 18, 2018, https://www.nbcnews.com/politics/first-read/new-election-map-ohio-colorado-no-longer-swing-states-n937646. States with high white populations and relatively low Hispanic and college-educated residents tend to vote Republican. The opposite is true for Democrats. *See ibid.*
24. Steven Shepard, "Poll: Voters Prefer Popular Vote Over Electoral College," *Politico*, March 27, 2019, https://www.politico.com/story/2019/03/27/poll-popular-vote-electoral-college-1238346.
25. Christopher Ingraham, "Elizabeth Warren Wants to Abolish the Electoral College. Here's How It Could Actually Happen—Sort Of," *Washington Post*, March 19, 2019, https://www.washingtonpost.com/us-policy/2019/03/19/elizabeth-warren-wants-abolish-electoral-college-heres-how-it-could-actually-happen-sort/?utm_term=.a216d765279b.
26. Akhil Reed Amar, "Some Thoughts on the Electoral College: Past, Present, and Future," *Ohio Northern University Law Review* 33, no. 2 (2007): 468–69.
27. Amar, "Some Thoughts on the Electoral College," 470, quoting Max Farrand, ed., *The Records of the Federal Convention of 1787*, rev. ed. (New Haven, Yale University Press, 1937, 1966; July 19, 1787), 57.
28. Ibid.

CHAPTER 7: Key Ingredients to Electing People to Congress

1. "United States House of Representatives," Ballotpedia, https://ballotpedia.org/United_States_House_of_Representatives.
2. U.S. Const., Article. 1, §§ 2, 4, 5.
3. Dep't of Commerce v. New York, 139 S. Ct. 953 (2019).
4. Garrett Epps, "A Supreme Court Case That Will Affect Every Aspect of National Life," *Atlantic*, April 21, 2019, https://www.theatlantic.com/ideas/archive/2019/04/can-census-ask-about-citizenship/587503/.
5. Matthew A. Baum, Bryce J. Dietrich, Rebecca Goldstein, and Maya Sen, "Estimating the Effect of Asking About Citizenship on the U.S. Census:

Results from a Randomized Controlled Trial," HKS Faculty Research Working Paper Series RWP19-015, April 2019, available at https://scholar.harvard.edu/files/mbaum/files/baum_et_al_citizenship_question.pdf.
6. Thomas B. Edsall, "Why Aren't Democrats Winning the Hispanic Vote 80–20 or 90–10?," *New York Times*, April 3, 2019, https://www.nytimes.com/2019/04/03/opinion/latino-voters.html.
7. "1790 Census," *National Geographic*, accessed June 16, 2019, https://www.nationalgeographic.org/media/us-census-1790; "Decennial Census of Population and Housing: By Decade," United States Census Bureau, accessed June 16, 2019, https://www.census.gov/programs-surveys/decennial-census/decade.2010.html.
8. "Members of Congress," govtrack, accessed June 15, 2019, https://www.govtrack.us/congress/members. This site allows users to enter their home addresses to find out who represents them in Congress and what bills their representatives have sponsored.
9. "Historical Highlights: The Permanent Apportionment Act of 1929," History, Art & Archives: United States House of Representatives, accessed June 16, 2019, https://history.house.gov/Historical-Highlights/1901–1950/The-Permanent-Apportionment-Act-of-1929/; Bruce Bartlett, "Enlarging the House of Representatives," *Economix*, January 7, 2014, https://economix.blogs.nytimes.com/2014/01/07/enlarging-the-house-of-representatives/.
10. *Encyclopaedia Britannica Online*, "United States House of Representatives Seats by State," https://www.britannica.com/topic/United-States-House-of-Representatives-Seats-by-State-1787120.
11. "Direct Election of Senators," United States Senate, https://www.senate.gov/artandhistory/history/common/briefing/Direct_Election_Senators.htm.
12. "The Senate and the United States Constitution," United States Senate, https://www.senate.gov/artandhistory/history/common/briefing/Constitution_Senate.htm.
13. "President Pro Tempore," United States Senate, https://www.senate.gov/artandhistory/history/common/briefing/President_Pro_Tempore.htm.
14. "United States Senate Elections, 2018," Ballotpedia, https://ballotpedia.org/United_States_Senate_elections,_2018.
15. Kathy Gill, "Filling Vacancies in the U.S. Senate," ThoughtCo., November 12, 2012, https://www.thoughtco.com/how-are-senate-vacancies-filled-3368245.
16. "Special Elections to the 116th United States Congress (2019–2020)," Bal-

lotpedia, https://ballotpedia.org/Special_elections_to_the_116th_United_States_Congress_(2019–2020).

Chapter 8: How Dug in Are Politicians? Gerrymandering and Limitless Terms for Congress

1. Scott Bomboy, "How the 22nd Amendment Came into Existence," Constitution Center, April 5, 2019, https://constitutioncenter.org/blog/how-the-22nd-amendment-came-into-existence.
2. Rucho v. Common Cause, 138 S. Ct. 923 (2019). For the full Supreme Court opinion see https://www.supremecourt.gov/opinions/18pdf/18–422_9ol1.pdf.
3. Reynolds v. Sims, 377 U.S. 533 (1964).
4. Rucho v. Common Cause, 138 S. Ct. 923 (2019).
5. Shaw v. Reno, 509 U.S. 630 (1993). For a summary of other significant Supreme Court cases on congressional districting, see "Redistricting and the Supreme Court: The Most Significant Cases," NCSL, April 25, 2019, http://www.ncsl.org/research/redistricting/redistricting-and-the-supreme-court-the-most-significant-cases.aspx.
6. "Independent Redistricting Commissions," Ballotpedia, accessed June 15, 2019, https://ballotpedia.org/Independent_redistricting_commissions; Arizona State Legislature v. Arizona Independent Redistricting Commission, 135 S. Ct. 2652 (2015).
7. Tom Murse, "The Debate Over Term Limits for Congress: The Pros and Cons of Imposing Term Limits for Congress," ThoughtCo., May 25, 2019, https://www.thoughtco.com/debate-over-term-limits-for-congress-3367505; Casey Burgat, "Five Reasons to Oppose Congressional Term Limits," Brookings, January 18, 2018, https://www.brookings.edu/blog/fixgov/2018/01/18/five-reasons-to-oppose-congressional-term-limits/.

Chapter 9: Does Your Vote Even Matter? Senate Malapportionment and Winner-Takes-All Vote Counting

1. Nate Cohn, "The Electoral College's Real Problem: It's Biased Toward the Big Battlegrounds," *New York Times*, March 22, 2019, https://www.nytimes.com/2019/03/22/upshot/electoral-college-votes-states.html.
2. "The Senate and the United States Constitution," United States Senate, Art & History, https://www.senate.gov/artandhistory/history/common/briefing/Constitution_Senate.htm.
3. Eric W. Orts, "The Path to Give California 12 Senators, and Vermont Just One," *Atlantic*, January 2, 2019, https://www.theatlantic.com/ideas/archive/2019/01/heres-how-fix-senate/579172/.

4. "This Day in History, August 8, 1974: Nixon Resigns," History .com, August 8, 2019, https://www.history.com/this-day-in-history/nixon-resigns.
5. Michael J. Gerhardt, "The Historical and Constitutional Significance of the Impeachment and Trial of President Clinton," *Hofstra Law Review* 28, no. 2 (1999): 365.
6. Nathaniel Rakich, "Democrats' Horrible 2018 Senate Map Couldn't Have Come at a Better Time," FiveThirtyEight, May 1, 2018, https://fivethirtyeight.com/features/democrats-horrible-2018-senate-map-couldnt-have-come-at-a-better-time/; *see also* Geoffrey R. Stone, "Who Controls the Senate Controls the Courts," *Daily Beast*, April 14, 2017, https://www.thedailybeast.com/who-controls-the-senate-controls-the-courts.
7. John Myers, "Radical Plan to Split California into Three States Earns Spot on November Ballot," *Los Angeles Times*, June 12, 2018, https://www.latimes.com/politics/la-pol-ca-california-split-three-states-20180612-story.html.
8. Rob Richie and Devin McCarthy, "Blame It on Winner-Take-All: Why Our Outdated Voting Rules Cause Congressional Crises," *Huffington Post*, October 1, 2013, updated January 23, 2014, https://www.huffpost.com/entry/blame-it-on-winner-take-a_b_4025860.
9. "Frequently Asked Questions," National Archives and Records Administration: U.S. Electoral College, https://www.archives.gov/federal-register/electoral-college/faq.html#wtapv.
10. "Types of Voting Systems," FairVote, https://www.fairvote.org/types_of_voting_systems.
11. Matthew Yglesias, "Proportional Representation Could Save America," Vox, October 15, 2018, https://www.vox.com/policy-and-politics/2018/10/15/17979210/proportional-representation-could-save-america.
12. Tara Law, "These Presidents Won the Electoral College—But Not the Popular Vote," *Time*, May 15, 2019, https://time.com/5579161/presidents-elected-electoral-college/.
13. "National Popular Vote, What It Is–Why It's Needed," National Popular Vote, Inc., https://www.nationalpopularvote.com.
14. Debra Cassens Weiss, "Winner-Take-All Electoral College System Is Unconstitutional, Say Suits Led by Boies," *ABA Journal*, February 22, 2018, http://www.abajournal.com/news/article/winner-take-all_electoral_college_system_is_unconstitutional_say_suits_by_b.
15. David Deschamps, Leslie D. Farrell, and Bennett Singer, *Electoral Dys-*

function (2012; Trio Pictures and The Center for Independent Documentary), http://electoraldysfunction.org.

Chapter 10: Money in Politics

1. Citizens United v. FEC, 558 U.S. 310 (2010); Gabrielle Levy, "How Citizens United Has Changed Politics in 5 Years," *U.S. News & World Report*, January 21, 2015. https://www.usnews.com/news/articles/2015/01/21/5-years-later-citizens-united-has-remade-us-politics.
2. "The FEC and the Federal Campaign Finance Law," Federal Election Commission, February 2004, https://transition.fec.gov/pages/brochures/fecfeca.shtml.
3. Peter Overby, "Beyond Quid Pro Quo: What Counts as Political Corruption?," NPR, It's All Politics, May 4, 2015, https://www.npr.org/sections/itsallpolitics/2015/05/04/404052618/beyond-quid-pro-quo-what-counts-as-political-corruption.
4. Citizens United v. FEC, 558 U.S. 310 (2010); "Making Independent Expenditures," Federal Election Commission, https://www.fec.gov/help-candidates-and-committees/making-independent-expenditures/.
5. Citizens United v. FEC, 558 U.S. 310 (2010); Levy, "How Citizens United Has Changed Politics in 5 Years."
6. 52 U.S.C.A. § 30116(a)(1)(A); "The FEC and the Federal Campaign Finance Law."
7. 11 C.F.R. § 110.11; *see generally* Kaitlin Washburn, "The Legacy and Impact of McCain-Feingold," OpenSecrets.org, August 28, 2018, https://www.opensecrets.org/news/2018/08/the-legacy-of-mccain-feingold/.
8. 52 U.S.C.A. § 30116(a)(1)(C). *See also* Fed. Election Comm'n Adv. Op. 2010–09.
9. "Political Action Committees," Center for Responsive Politics, https://www.opensecrets.org/pacs/.
10. "Political Action Committees, Super PACs," Center for Responsive Politics, https://www.opensecrets.org/pacs/superpacs.php?cycle=2020.
11. Ibid.
12. 26 U.S.C.A. § 527.
13. "Campaign Finance," National Conference of State Legislatures, accessed October 26, 2019, http://www.ncsl.org/research/elections-and-campaigns/ncsl-s-campaign-finance-webpages.aspx#Other.
14. "All Commissioners," Federal Election Commission, accessed October 26, 2019, https://www.fec.gov/about/leadership-and-structure/commissioners/.

Chapter 11: Voter Suppression and Voter Fraud: Myths or Realities?

1. John Lewis, "Now We Know That Not All Votes Count," *New York Times*, December 2, 2000, https://www.nytimes.com/2000/12/02/opinion/now-we-know-that-not-all-votes-count.html?searchResultPosition=1.
2. Shelby County v. Holder, 570 U.S. 529, 557 (2013).
3. 52 U.S.C.A. § 20511.
4. P. R. Lockhart, "Stacey Abrams's Fight for Voting Rights Matters More Than Her Political Future," Vox, August 30, 2019, https://www.vox.com/policy-and-politics/2019/8/30/20838979/stacey-abrams-voting-rights-suppression-fair-fight-2020.
5. "Elections," Georgia Secretary of State, https://sos.ga.gov/index.php/elections; Alan Blinder, "Brian Kemp Resigns as Georgia Secretary of State, with Governor's Race Still Disputed," *New York Times*, November 8, 2018, https://www.nytimes.com/2018/11/08/us/georgia-brian-kemp-resign-stacey-abrams.html?module=inline.
6. Fair Fight Action v. Crittenden, Complaint for Declaratory and Injunctive Relief, accessed February 13, 2020, https://webcache.googleusercontent.com/search?q=cache:OepLh3JtUbIJ:https://moritzlaw.osu.edu/electionlaw/litigation/documents/FFAC1.pdf+&cd=1&hl=en&ct=clnk&gl=us&client=safari
7. Ibid.
8. Johnny Kauffman, "Georgia Governor Signs Law to Slow 'Use It or Lose It' Voter Purges," *APM Reports*, April 11, 2019, https://www.apmreports.org/story/2019/04/11/georgia-brian-kemp-use-it-or-lose-it-voting-law-changes.
9. "Georgia Election Results," *Washington Post*, April 6, 2019, https://www.washingtonpost.com/election-results/georgia/.
10. Shelby County v. Holder, 570 U.S. 2 (2013); *see generally* Stephanie N. Kang, "Restoring the Fifteenth Amendment: The Constitutional Right to an Undiluted Vote," *U.C.L.A. Law Review* 62, no. 5 (2015): 1392 (observing that the Supreme Court has not "honor[ed] the Fifteenth Amendment's robust protections of minority voting rights").
11. Miriam Valverde, "Georgia's 'Exact Match' Law and the Abrams-Kemp Governor's Election, Explained," Politifact, October 19, 2018, https://www.politifact.com/georgia/article/2018/oct/19/georgias-exact-match-law-and-its-impact-voters-gov/.
12. "Resources on Voter Fraud Claims," Brennan Center for Justice, June 26, 2017, https://www.brennancenter.org/our-work/research-reports/resources-voter-fraud-claims.

13. Justin Levitt, "The Truth About Voter Fraud," Brennan Center for Justice, November 9, 2007, https://www.brennancenter.org/our-work/research-reports/truth-about-voter-fraud.
14. "New Voting Restrictions in America," Brennan Center for Justice, October 1, 2019, https://www.brennancenter.org/new-voting-restrictions-america.
15. Christopher Ingraham, "Thousands of Polling Places Were Closed Over the Past Decade. Here's Where," *Washington Post*, October 28, 2018, https://www.washingtonpost.com/business/2018/10/26/thousands-polling-places-were-closed-over-past-decade-heres-where/.

Chapter 12: Voter Misinformation: A Primer on Foreign Interference in U.S. Presidential Elections

1. Matt Rhoades, "US Elections Are Under Threat from Cyberattacks—And So Are Yours," *Politico*, May 21, 2018, https://www.politico.eu/article/all-elections-under-threat-cyberattacks/; Laura Daniels, "How Russia Hacked the French Election," *Politico*, April 23, 2017, https://www.politico.eu/article/france-election-2017-russia-hacked-cyberattacks/.
2. Philip Ewing, "What You Need to Know About Foreign Interference and the 2020 Election," NPR, September 1, 2019, https://www.npr.org/2019/09/01/737978684/what-you-need-to-know-about-foreign-interference-and-the-2020-election.
3. "Understanding Denial-of-Service Attacks," CISA, US Department of Homeland Security, June 28, 2018, https://www.us-cert.gov/ncas/tips/ST04-015; Charles Stewart III and Merle King, "A Cyberattack Could Disrupt Tuesday's U.S. Elections—But Wouldn't Change the Results," *Washington Post*, November 7, 2016, https://www.washingtonpost.com/news/monkey-cage/wp/2016/11/07/a-cyberattack-could-disrupt-tuesdays-u-s-elections-but-wouldnt-change-the-results/.
4. "The Phishing Email That Hacked the Account of John Podesta," CBS News, October 28, 2016, https://www.cbsnews.com/news/the-phishing-email-that-hacked-the-account-of-john-podesta/.
5. Christopher Bing, "Exclusive: U.S. Officials Fear Ransomware Attack Against 2020 Election," Reuters, August 26, 2019, https://www.reuters.com/article/us-usa-cyber-election-exclusive/exclusive-us-officials-fear-ransomware-attack-against-2020-election-idUSKCN1VG222.
6. Ian Millhiser, "The Astounding Advantage the Electoral College Gives to Republicans, in One Chart," Vox, September 17, 2019, https://www.vox

.com/policy-and-politics/2019/9/17/20868790/republicans-lose-popular-vote-win-electoral-college.

7. Select Committee On Intelligence, Report of the Select Committee on Intelligence United States Senate on Russian Active Measures Campaigns and Interference in the 2016 U.S. Election Volume 1: Russian Efforts Against Election Infrastructure with Additional Views, S. Rep. No. 116-XX, at 3 (2019), https://www.intelligence.senate.gov/sites/default/files/documents/Report_Volume1.pdf.
8. Carol Dexter, "Our Founding Fathers Wanted a Republic, Not a Democracy," Union, August 15, 2013, https://www.theunion.com/news/twi/our-founding-fathers-wanted-a-republic-not-a-democracy/.
9. Bess Lovejoy, "9 False Rumors with Real-Life Consequences," *Mental Floss*, January 15, 2018, http://mentalfloss.com/article/72892/9-false-rumors-real-life-consequences.
10. Scott Shane, "The Fake Americans Russia Created to Influence the Election," *New York Times*, September 7, 2017, https://www.nytimes.com/2017/09/07/us/politics/russia-facebook-twitter-election.html.
11. Laura Galante and Shaun Ee, "Defining Russian Election Interference: An Analysis of Select 2014 to 2018 Cyber Enabled Incidents," Atlantic Council, September 11, 2018, https://atlanticcouncil.org/wp-content/uploads/2018/09/Defining_Russian_Election_Interference_web.pdf.
12. Jack Crowe, "Senate Intel Committee Confirms Russians Hacked Election Systems in 50 States, Didn't Change Vote Totals, *National Review*, July 26, 2019, https://www.nationalreview.com/news/senate-intel-committee-confirms-russians-hacked-election-systems-in-50-states-didnt-change-vote-totals/.
13. "Election Security," CISA, US Department of Homeland Security, https://www.dhs.gov/cisa/election-security.
14. Kevin Collier, "DHS Moves to Defend City and State Voter Registration Databases from Ransomware Attacks," CNN Politics, August 26, 2019, https://www.cnn.com/2019/08/26/politics/dhs-cisa-voter-registration-ransomware/index.html.

Index